MW01628425

The History of New Hope, Virginia

The Past Two Hundred Years

By
Wayne Edward Garber
and
Owen Early Harner

Owen E. Harner

Lot's Wife Publishing
Staunton, Virginia

2006

Cover design by Jennifer Wood.
Interior layout by Nancy Sorrells.

Lot's Wife Publishing
P.O. Box 1844
Staunton, VA 24402
www.lotswifepublishing.com

Library of Congress Catalog Card Number 2006935318
ISBN-10 0-9752745-9-7
ISBN-13 978-0-9752745-9-0

To the New Hope Community:
past, present, & future

Table of Contents

Preface and Acknowledgments

As I was writing a family history, *Johannes "John H." Garber (1732-1787), A Branch of His Descendants*, I was unable to find any histories of New Hope, Virginia, that would assist me in my work. I approached Owen Harner for assistance and discovered that Owen was not aware of any New Hope history, but had been collecting newspaper articles and photographs about the community for over fifty years. Owen felt that New Hope had a wonderful and rich historical background that needed to be documented and shared. The village is located in the heart of the beautiful Shenandoah Valley and situated in the historic area of Augusta County. Although Owen and I are not historians, we have written *History of New Hope, Virginia*, to preserve some of its past heritage before it is gone forever.

The task of writing this book has been somewhat difficult because very little information seems to exist regarding New Hope's origin, buildings, or residents. The residents for the most part were not people in positions of power that appeared in the history books or left personal papers. Due to time and logistical considerations, we have not attempted to perform extensive research or interview many local residents. We do want to acknowledge individuals who helped by providing old photographs and relevant information. They are as follows: Whit Bauserman, Doris Borden, Julia Boward, Polly Brumfield, Elizabeth Campbell, Earline and Kelly Chapman, B. F. Caricofe, Jr., Donald Carpenter, Ralph Coffman, Juanita Curry, Vernon Davis, Dorothy Daughtry, Bob Daughtry, Sue Ervin, Leonard Early, Nellie Flora, Phyllis Fretwell, Gene Garber, Hazel Harner, Mildred Hartman, Rebecca Harvill, Virginia Hawkins, Lawrence Hildebrand, Esther Howdyshell, Bobby Kester, Vickie King, Jo Layman, John Lockridge, Mark Mehler, Mary Vernon Mowry, Joe Nutt, William and Sue Patterson, Glenna Powers, Mary Alice Roadcap, Billie Rosen, Irene Shorts, Mary Stout, Clairrine Veney, Mary Margaret Wampler, Ethel V. White, Isabell Willberger, Mac Wiseman, Nelson Young, and the Augusta County School system's central office.

Our objectives were twofold: first, to compile, organize, and summarize available information about New Hope and, second, to provide some additional documentation and historical background relating to the subject. We believe it is important that we not forget the past and the legacy of our forefathers. It is our hope that our efforts may help present and future generations understand and appreciate New Hope's rich and interesting heritage and create community interest in improving the quality of life in the village.

In compiling this work, we have used the sources and material that we felt would be most valuable and have tried to be as factual as possible. We made use of the books, reference works, and research archives held by the following Virginia institutions: the Library of Virginia in Richmond; Colonial Williamsburg Foundation's John D. Rockefeller, Jr. Library; the Augusta County Library at Fishersville; and the Augusta County Historical Society. We did not explore all the relevant documentary collections in the United States. What is offered here is a summary of primary and secondary sources, both old and new, supplemented by personal knowledge and family information.

Both authors apologize in advance for any inadvertent mistakes or errors of fact. So many individuals helped in the creation of this book that we are also certain that we have inadvertently omitted someone's name. Please consider this a blanket word of thanks for your help in preserving the heritage of the community of New Hope.

Wayne Edward Garber
and Owen Early Harner
October 2006

Historical Overview

The Shenandoah Valley lies between the Blue Ridge Mountains on the east and the Allegheny Mountains on the west. The village of New Hope is located in the heart of this beautiful valley about ten miles east of Staunton and nine miles northwest of Waynesboro, Virginia. The village of New Hope is also situated in the historic area of Augusta County near the confluence of Meadow Run (formerly Long Meadow Run and, before that, Beaver Run), Christians Creek, and Middle River (formerly Cathey's River).

Around 1700, English interest increased in the Shenandoah Valley as trade with the Indians was becoming very profitable and there was an increasing need for settlement to act as a buffer between the French and Indians to the west and the English in eastern Virginia. In 1716, more than a century after the founding of Jamestown, Governor Alexander Spotswood attempted the passage of the "Great Mountains" for the purpose of establishing Virginia's western claims. On a bright day in early September, Governor Spotswood reached the brow of a declivity at the top of the Blue Ridge Mountains and described the glorious sight as follows: "The broad valley spread out before them; miles of tall grass gently waved and shimmered in the September sun; huge patches of forest, whose foliage was just beginning to take on the mellow hues of Autumn, lent beauty and variety to the scene; the Shenandoah river wound in and out among the groves and grassy meadows like a broad thread of silver in a giant's cloth of green and gold; and off yonder, a dozen miles to the north, the bold extremity of the Massanutten Mountain came jutting out into the Valley, like some rugged headland in a quiet sea." He led his party of fifty strong, including gentlemen, servants, and Indian guides through what is now Swift Run Gap down into the Shenandoah Valley, where they crossed the river and buried on the other side a bottle containing a paper claiming all that territory for His Majesty King George I.

It was ten to fifteen years after the date of Spotswood's expedition that permanent settlements in the Great Valley of Virginia were made. By 1730, many German and Scotch-Irish began arriving from Pennsylvania and crossing the Potomac at what is now Shepherdstown, West Virginia. This settlement of the Shenandoah Valley was encouraged by Virginia's colonial government as a buffer against expanding French influence in the Ohio Valley.

In 1730, William Gooch, Governor of Virginia, granted 40,000 acres to Isaac Vanmeter in the Valley of Virginia. In 1732, an expedition led by Joist Hite came up the Valley to settle upon this grant. Among the settlers in this expedition was John Lewis who, together with his wife and children, settled further south and built a home about a mile east of the present city of Staunton. Lewis is one of the earliest documented settlers of Augusta County, but simultaneous to his family's arrival was that of the Kerr family, which settled in the New Hope area around 1732.

In 1736, William Beverley received an 118,491-acre land grant in consideration for inducing a large number of settlers to the upper Valley. The Beverley Manor grant embraced the site of the present city of Staunton and much of Augusta County. The land already settled by the Lewis and Kerr families was located in Beverley Manor and both families eventually purchased from Beverley the land on which they had already been living for several years.

By the year of 1738, so many settlers had emigrated from east of the mountains as well as from Pennsylvania, and from Europe, that the Virginia legislature needed to extend local government west of the Blue Ridge Mountains. As a result, Augusta County, named after the Princess of Wales, was created out of Orange County. Its boundaries extended from the Blue Ridge Mountains to the Mississippi River and south from the Great Lakes to North Carolina. For seven years, until 1745, government functions continued to emanate from Orange County. But by 1745, Augusta's population had increased enough that a local government could be formed. Beverley gave a small building at his Mill Place (as Staunton was first called) to be used as the county courthouse.

In Virginia at that time, there was no separation of church and state. The Church of England, today called the Episcopal Church, was an arm of the colonial government. As such, everyone in the county paid taxes to help build a church and employ an Anglican minister who was part of the local governing body located in Staunton. Presbyterians, having left the north of Ireland to escape paying dues to the Church of England, were among the first to come to the Shenandoah Valley. In addition to the Presbyterians, there were active congregations of Germans, mostly Lutheran and Reformed congregations but also a smattering of Anabaptists. As Dissenters, these groups were granted religious tolerance under Virginia's colonial government, but were still required to be official participants in the Anglican Church. Dissenters could have their own houses of worship, which had to be called meeting houses not churches, but they still paid taxes to help build the Augusta Parish Church in Staunton and hire a minister.

In the New Hope area, many of the Dissenters were German-speaking families including a group of Anabaptists, called Dunkers (for their practice of fully immersing adults during baptism) or later known as the Church of the Brethren. It is known that Dunkers were settled on Christians Creek by 1750, with even larger settlements farther north on the lower bottom land of Middle River and in the Crimora area, approximately six miles from New Hope, before 1790. These pioneers settled on the fertile soil along Middle River. Just like other Valley settlers, they had to brave the dangers of the wilderness and worked hard to clear the land, build their homes, and produce their food and other necessities.

Looking down the New Hope Road, photograph taken circa 1850.

Looking up the New Hope Road from the opposite direction as the photograph above.

New Hope Historical Timeline

Date	Event
1716	Governor Alexander Spotswood's Expedition crossed the Blue Ridge Mountains to the Shenandoah Valley for the purpose of establishing Virginia's western claims.
1732	Joist Hite Expedition came up the Valley and among the settlers in this expedition was John Lewis, who settled much further south and built his home about a mile east of the present city of Staunton.
1732	The James Kerr family settled in the New Hope area.
1736	William Beverley received an 118,491-acre land grant, which embraced the site of the present city of Staunton.
1738	The Virginia General Assembly established Augusta County (carved out of Orange County) with its boundaries extending from the Blue Ridge Mountains to the Mississippi River and south from the Great Lakes to North Carolina.
1730-40s	James Kerr (1696-1770), reputed progenitor of most of Augusta County's Kerr families, built a home near the points of confluence of Long Meadow Run, Christians Creek, and Middle River.
1750	Dunkers (Also called Tunkers, German Baptist, and Church of the Brethren) settled on Christians Creek.
1784	Edward Rutledge (1725–1786) built Black Oak Spring or the Rutledge-Mehler House, which is one of the oldest brick houses in the New Hope area.
1790-92	William Beard built the original part of the Belmont Plantation house, a four-room log house.
1790	Dr. James Allen was New Hope's first doctor, who practiced medicine in the area until the late 1830s.
1804	James M. Stout built a brick general merchandise store, which was New Hope's first public building.
1809	The first house of worship in the New Hope community was the old log building known as the Round Hill Meeting House, which represents the beginnings of the New Hope United Methodist Church.
1818	The Dickerson Tavern, New Hope's second known public building, was built as a tavern and stagecoach stop, which provided lodging, food, and rest for guests.
1820-30s	The village grew slowly with the building of more houses on New Hope Road near the Stout General Merchandise Store and the Dickerson-Fretwell Tavern.
1824	Abraham Garber was instrumental in building the first Dunker Church in Augusta County and the second oldest Brethren Church in Virginia on his farm. The church is known today as the Middle River Church of the Brethren.
1829	New Hope postal operations were established in the New Hope General Merchandise Store.

1830s	The Humbert-Knightly mill dam was built before July 1833 and the mill and sawmill were built shortly thereafter.
1830-40s	Dr. G. W. McCullogh was the New Hope area's second doctor, who practiced medicine in the village in the late 1830s to early 1840s
1840s	Myers-Bauserman Shops established (wheelwright, blacksmith, and paint shops).
1840s	The New Hope Town Hall was built and was the first example of a building called a "town hall" in Augusta County.
1845	Dr. William Roberts built a house on his 100+ acre farmstead.
1864	At the Battle of Piedmont, the U.S. Army of General David Hunter crushed the smaller Confederate Army, killing the C.S.A. commander (General "Grumble" Jones) and taking nearly 1,000 prisoners.
1864	The original Humbert-Knightly mill building was burned by Civil War General Philip Sheridan's northern soldiers during the Valley's scorched earth campaign.
1870	The Ft. Defiance mill was established on Middle River, near where Route 616 (Dam Town Road) crosses Middle River.
1870	The East Augusta Mutual Insurance Company was formed in New Hope by farmers, who were vitally interested in protecting their homes and farm properties.
1870	After the Civil War, a mandatory free statewide public school system was created in Virginia. New Hope's first two public schoolhouses were two- or three-room white frame buildings; one built on or near the present school site and the other, for African-American students, at Round Hill. The first school session for both schools began in September of 1870
1870	The Mt. Tabor Church, a v-notched log structure, was built and is the oldest surviving black church in Augusta County. The congregation was established in 1841.
1870	The Fretwell barn, which was located in the heart of New Hope, was built.
1874	The first (New Hope area) train traveled from Pleasant Valley, just south of Harrisonburg, to Staunton on March 18, 1874. Historically, the line began as the Valley Railroad Company of Virginia with Robert E. Lee serving as its first president.
1880	The Willberger bank barn, located behind the Dickerson-Fretwell Tavern, was built.
1882	New Hope was the largest village in the present Middle River District and was the fifth largest community in Augusta County.
1880s	The Ft. Defiance Railway Depot began operations by shipping flour and bringing fertilizer to New Hope area farmers.
1890	The town of New Hope was incorporated with the passage of Senate Bill No. 144 by the Virginia General Assembly.
c1890	The New Hope Presbyterian Chapel was built as an outreach of Old Stone Presbyterian Church, which is located in Ft. Defiance.

1892	The Willberger farmstead, one mile south of New Hope, was built.
1892	Willberger Funeral Service was founded by William "Willie" Henry Willberger and was one of two funeral homes in the northern end of Augusta County.
1898-99	The Kerr Crossing Bridge, which carries Route 907 across Christians Creek near the old Kerr house, was built.
1902	The New Hope Switch Board Association was founded and began providing telephone services from H. C. Anthony's house, which is across the street from the present telephone company location.
1905	A second-generation New Hope school building, a two-storied white-framed structure, was built.
1906	Robert Odie Willberger and his partner, C. D. Crawford, started the Crawford and Willberger Store, a general store located in the center of New Hope.
1912	The New Hope Road was macadamized (paved) and a toll house was built at the corner of Routes 608 and west 616 for collecting tolls from New Hope to Ft. Defiance. New Hope became unincorporated.
1913	The Bank of New Hope was built and opened for business.
1915	The Knightly Steel Truss Bridge (STB), which carries Route 778 across Middle River just south of Knightly, was built.
1916	The Humbert-Knightly mill installed two dynamos to generate electricity and began to build an electrical distribution system in the Mt. Sidney, Ft. Defiance, and New Hope areas.
1918	Homer Early applied for and received an authorized Lincoln, Ford, and Fordson Tractors dealership. The repair shop and dealership was called the New Hope Garage.
1918	The Mt. Bethel Baptist Church at Round Hill was built.
1924	The New Hope brick school building was erected as a high school and the frame building became the elementary school.
1925	Wine's Service Station, located beside the Live Wire Garage, opened.
1928	Crossroads (Paxton's) Service Station opened for business.
1930	The Livewire Garage was constructed and opened for business.
1932	The first community fair was held but the annual event was suspended at the beginning of WWII.
1938	Walter Scrogham's Service Station, across from the New Hope School, opened for business.
1939	The organizational meeting of the New Hope Ruritan Club was conducted on March 14.
1943	Mac Wiseman, country music legend, graduated from New Hope High School.
1946	An early-morning blaze razed New Hope's white-frame 'grammar school building.
1947	Wine's Service Station was closed and converted to a residence.
1951	The New Hope Troop 86 received its Boy Scouts of America charter.

1952 New Hope dedicated its new Medical Center and handed the keys to the building to Dr. William T. Davis.
1965 The New Hope Medical Center was closed because the community was unable to attract a new doctor.
1965 The Middle River Church of the Brethren built a new sanctuary. They later added a social hall in 1974.
1965 The Ft. Defiance Depot was closed and the railroad right-of-way from Harrisonburg to Staunton was sold to a private concern.
1975 The New Hope Garage and New Hope General Store were closed.
1977 The New Hope United Methodist Church built a new sanctuary.
1979 Willberger's Funeral Service, which operated for nearly 100 years, was closed.
1980 The Crawford and Willberger Store was closed after more than seventy years of operation.
1981 New Hope was included on Virginia's highway map.
1980s Augusta County brought sewer service to New Hope.
1990 The New Hope Volunteer Fire Department was established.
1990 The Bank of New Hope was closed.
1995 The New Hope School was closed.
1999 Rankin Station, home of the New Hope Volunteer Fire Department, was built.

Perhaps no picture better sums up the richness of New Hope community life when the school was the center of activity. In 1939, this group presented a play, ***Mystery at Midnight****, to raise funds for a school piano. Pictured here is a cross section of area citizens, including community physician Dr. Theron Rolston, teachers, high school principals, students, farmers, and the "Hungry Five," a five-piece band made up of (L-R) Harry Kerr, Boyd Thompson, Jr., Homer Crickenberger, Roy Geiman, and Kelly Chapman, as well as all the high school students.*

Historical Houses

Kerr House

Take Laurel Hill Road (Virginia 612) east from the traffic light on U.S. 11 in Verona and proceed 4.2 miles (located two miles west of New Hope). There, on your left, perched on a hill well above Middle River, you'll see the Old Kerr House, a log building now sheathed in clapboard with a large central stone chimney that ranks among the oldest standing homes in the upper Valley. It is situated near the points of confluence of Long Meadow (formerly Gearer, then Beaver) Run, Christians (formerly Thirsty, then Christie) Creek, and Middle (formerly Catheys) River. Kerr family legend states that the house, or a portion of it incorporated in the present structure, was built between 1730 and 1740 by James Kerr, reputed progenitor of most of Augusta County's Kerr families. However, no dendrochronology (dating houses by examining tree rings) has been conducted to confirm this story.

The Kerrs, the first known settlers in the New Hope area, constructed a portion of this house in the eighteenth century.

We consulted Vincent Brown Kerr's book entitled *Brief History of Kerrs and Kin, 1730-1930,* published in Staunton in 1930. From this source we derived the following information: "The records of Augusta County give many ways the Kerr name is spelled, as follows: Car, Care, Carr, Carre, Ceer, Kare, Keer, Kear, Kearr, Ker, and Kerr." As Kerr, usually pronounced Carr, is the predominant and most current and generally used form, we retain it here. Vincent Kerr traces the Kerrs through Scotland and Ireland into Pennsylvania, probably Lancaster County, down into Augusta and the Middle River area in the 1730s and 1740s. This first James Kerr (1696-1770) and his eldest son John may have settled at the old Kerr homesite as early as 1730, by some accounts, which would have placed them in the area before the John Lewis settlement farther south. And they may have held title to the land by royal patent, as family tradition recounts, although we know of no tangible proof or verification of this.

The northeast corner of the Beverley Manor grant was established by survey in 1736 on the Kerr property. The stone marking this corner was discovered not far from this house by William McCue in 1908 and now rests in the Augusta County Courthouse. The deed for this property from William Beverley to John Kerr was recorded on August 19, 1752. These early deeds were often negotiated years or even decades after initial settlement, so there is no indication that James Kerr and his family were not on the site in the 1730s. James Kerr is on record as being one of the justices of the first court held in Staunton in 1745, and he was an elder in the Tinkling Spring Presbyterian Church. In the early 1740s, branches of the Kerr family were settling in the present Kerrs Creek area, and in the 1780s in the Summerdean area, west of Middlebrook, according to Vincent Kerr. James Kerr bought additional tracts of land over the years, with his ultimate holdings exceeding 1,000 acres. John Kerr and his descendants - and some of the Kerr families were very large - also acquired large tracts. With time, Kerr lands extended well up present Long Meadow Run, along large segments of Middle River, and westward beyond present U.S. 11.

The Kerrs were among the families that built Augusta Stone Presbyterian Church, and many Kerr children were baptized by the Rev. John Craig, the first settled minister in the upper Valley. Members of the Kerr family migrated westward from the mid-eighteenth century, and others married into prominent Augusta families, many of whom yet reside in this area. To name a few of the families that became interrelated with the Kerrs over the years: Forrer, Revercomb, Hogshead, McClure, Ramsey, Dunlap, Smith, Bell, Armentrout, Dixon, Sites, Robertson, Coiner/Koiner, Overall, Coffman, Drumheller, Cline, Opie, Jones, Timberlake, Waddell, Patterson, Nutt, Armstrong, McCutcheon, Rosen, Wallace, Mercer, Hoge, McCorkle, McPherson, Hanna, Sproul, and Swisher.

An architectural survey conducted on the house by the Virginia Landmarks Commission in 1982 by Ann McCleary concluded that the original dwelling included the present three rooms east of the central chimney. The house faces generally south, so this would include the portion to the right of the chimney in the sketch. The survey continues: "Structural evidence shows that the log walls of the west section are butted against notched walls of the east section, indicating a later date of construction for the west section, although the latter is also quite old." While the interior has been remodeled, the commission report indicates the parts of the home that confirm a very early date of construction, including: most of the flooring and some trim; finely beaded exposed floor joists and girts; beaded board partitions dividing some of the rooms; the large stone chimney, which measures eight feet by four feet, with two opposing fireplaces, each capable of holding six-foot backlogs; a partial stone-walled root cellar on the east end of the house accessible through a trapdoor opening on the porch and stone steps descending to it; and two doors, including a board and batten front door with strap hinges, and a raised four-panel door leading into the older section.

An 1880 photograph of the house in Vincent Kerr's book indicates that there have been few exterior changes in the basic structure over the last 110 years. In 1880, there was, however, a large log building, reportedly a kitchen wing and also perhaps a slave quarters, attached to the east end of the house, and the roofline west of the chimney was somewhat lower than that of the east side.

The home apparently remained in the Kerr family for about 230 years and through seven generations. The commission's survey designates the chain of title from William Beverley to John Kerr, 1752; to William Mathews, 1761; James Agnew, 1784; James Kerr, 1788; John Kerr, 1803; J. Kerr Heirs to Col. Nathaniel Kerr, 1849; Vincent B. Kerr, 1895; and Walter Lee and Maude Kerr, 1904. In early 1950s, the home and nearly nineteen acres were purchased by Kenneth Landram, Sr., and his wife Audrey from Mrs. Walter (Maude) Kerr. Landram says that Mrs. Kerr's daughter, Mrs. Russell (Dorothy) Kerr Swisher, was residing there at the time and that she had extensively remodeled the interior of the home. The Landrams have altered the home very little during their residency of more than forty years. Landram retired in 1985 after thirty-seven years with Du Pont in Waynesboro.

The Kerrs operated at least one sawmill and adjacent gristmill near the home site from 1903 or earlier. Remains of early mill dams and the foundations of old mills can be seen today along all three of the waterways that converge within 150 yards of the house, and a number of these undoubtedly were Kerr properties at one time.

SOURCES: For additional information on the Old Kerr House, see the article in the *Augusta Historical Bulletin*, Vol. 8, No. 2, Fall 1972, by Gladys B. Clem. Mrs. Robert (Mary Beirne Kerr) Nutt contributed to the genealogical and other information included in this article; Ann McCleary, Historic Resources in Augusta County, Va., "Eighteenth Century to the Present, Historic Landmarks of Virginia" (now Department of Historic Resources), 1982; Joe Nutt, *Daily News Leader,* October 28, 1992.

Black Oak Spring/Rutledge-Mehler House

Black Oak Spring or the Rutledge-Mehler is one of the oldest brick houses in the New Hope/Ft. Defiance area. The original 1749 land grant was to James Kerr and an early name for the property was "Flag Spring." In 1753, Kerr sold 250 acres to Edward Rutledge, who was born in Ireland about 1725, immigrating to America around 1735-40. He married Sarah Armstrong and the couple had six children. Rutledge purchased twenty-six additional acres, with (an earlier) house in 1762. In 1784, he gave half of his property to his son James. It is believed, but not proven, that the Rutledges built this manor house on or about that year. In 1786, the year he died, Edward gave the remaining (eastern) half of the property to his son George.

In 1800, James Rutledge and Christian Arehart (Earhart) sold his property to David Rife who, in turn, sold it to Jacob Fischer in 1807. Jacob and Mary

Black Oak Spring/Rutledge-Mehler House, circa 1784

Fischer (Fisher) sold it to John Garber, in 1837, Garber heirs – Benjamin, Elizabeth, Elias, Susan, and John – sold it to Samuel Garber. Samuel Garber's heirs sold it to James M. Stout in 1874, whose heirs, in 1889, sold the property to W. H. and I. S. Humbert. Sadie Scrogham, a niece of Humbert, acquired the farm by will in 1900.

It was sold in 1940 to Hobart Earman, who sold it in 1945 to A. J. and Hilda Mehler. A. J., a student of history, had a keen interest in his house and land, and learned that the Humberts operated the mill on the property. The mill burned down in the early 1960s. A. J. also found that a portion of the George Rutledge land (the eastern section, near present Battlefield Rd., "had been donated for a Presbyterian or Lutheran meeting house sometime after 1800." Ann McCleary notes that "no foundations for the building remain; a burial plot with unidentified marble stones survives. This was used mostly by the Eakles." The Reverend Nat G. Barnhart writes in his history of the New Hope United Methodist Church that the earliest name of the church to be found in documented papers (county deed books) was "the Round Hill Meeting House," on land deeded (donated) by James Kerr and George Rutledge, land which was to include a school and burying ground "to the only proper use for Lutheran and Presbyterian Societies, German and English." The deed was dated March 27, 1809.

In 1839, this meeting house congregation was combined with the Providence Meeting House as a single charge by 1870; the combination is listed as the Methodist Episcopal Church, later becoming Round Hill and Methodist Church, South. The three branches of Methodism united in 1939 and after the 1968 union with the Evangelical United Brethren Church, became the present New Hope United Methodist Church.

Albert J. Mehler, Jr., passed away in 1991 and his wife Hilda in 1992, and the Black Oak Spring property was inherited by their son Marc J. Mehler. Marc is in the process of restoring the house to near-original condition, has removed the destructive ivy illustrated in the drawing, and will eliminate some of the later additions.

SOURCES: Joe Nutt provided written information to Owen Harner.

Belmont Plantation/Beard House

The farm known as Belmont (Farm or Plantation) is situated on the southern edge of this village on Route 608 or Battlefield Road just south of its junction with Patterson Mill Road (Va. 778). It is on the waters of Givens Mill Run which flows into nearby Middle River. For six generations, Belmont has been the home of members of the Beard family, starting with William Beard, who bought portions of the property in 1784, and extending through William's son

James P. Beard, James' sons David and Samuel Beard, David's son Gleaves C. Beard, Sr., Gleaves' son Gleaves C. Beard, Jr., and the latter's children Gleaves C. Beard III and Esther Beard Howdyshell. In 1971, Gleaves C. Beard III conveyed his half interest in the property to his brother-in-law and sister, Doyle W. and Esther (Beard) Howdyshell.

William Beard became a large landowner and prosperous farmer. He built the original part of the present home, a four-room log house, in 1790 to 1792. Upon his death in 1834 or early 1835, he left a great deal of real and personal property to his wife and sons. A partial inventory of his estate can be found in the book *My Augusta – A Spot of Earth, Not a Woman* by C. E. May, Good Printers, Bridgewater, Va., 1987.

A distillery had operated on the farm for some time, but apparently became a more sizable commercial operation under David Beard, William's grandson. According to May, "David Beard operated the distillery under the firm name Beard & Finley (with a neighboring farmer named Finley) during the 1870s and 1880s. Records of the estate show $1,000 in credits received from the sale of whiskey. The firm was registered in the Sixth Collection District of Virginia (state licensed) as No. 167. The brick chimney of the distillery still stands at Belmont, and the steel plate and stencil bearing the words "Whiskey, New Hope, Va." is in the possession of the Howdyshells."

Belmont Plantation-Beard House, built circa 1790-92

Belmont Plantation-Beard House, picture taken 1905

The property expanded and diminished over the years, at one time exceeding 1,400 acres, as the house enlarged in size under successive owners. According to Katherine Bushman in an article on Belmont in the *Augusta Historical Bulletin*, Vol. 6, No. 2, Fall 1969: "After the Civil War, the slave quarters were razed and a new ell built on the east side of the house. The front of the house faced north (the high columns built in 1839) toward a road that is no longer there. In 1910, Va. 608 was constructed (improved) and a 'front' on the west side of the house (the right side in the sketch) was created by adding another single-story porch. There are 14 rooms with a stairwell from the first floor to the attic. The attic also contains three rooms. The ceiling in the front room was painted by a traveling church decorator, Robert Green, in 1830, when he was forced to stop with 'horse trouble' (a lame mount) at Belmont. It was painted freehand and the design missed the exact center of the room by a mere two inches. The colors of red, blue, and gold are as vivid today as they were in 1830. The only ceiling which has been replaced is the one in the front hall, and that was due to stains caused by hiding hams, shoulders, and sides in it during the Civil War."

C. E. May adds to the description: "The floors throughout the house are made of pine boards six inches wide. The doors are of Crusader design, and many of them still have the original hardware. There are fireplaces in each (major) room, the largest one in the dining room. One side of it is flanked by a door to the kitchen, the other by a closet connecting the dining room and kitchen."

"Belmont is full of furniture used by generations of Beards who have dwelt in the manor house. A heavy walnut bedroom suite, including a four-poster bed, a dresser, a wash bowl, and a baby bed decorated with hand-carved pineapples are only a few of the many heirlooms in the house prized by the Howdyshells. The baby bed has served at least five generation of Beards."

Gladys B. Clem, in an article in *Augusta Historical Bulletin*, Vol. 7, No. 1, Spring 1971, writes of the Civil War Battle of Piedmont that swirled around the home: "A little 6-year-old boy sat on a tree-shaded hill that overlooked his father's farm. The June morning was hot and sultry, with a deep haze that nearly obscured the sun. In the distance, flames sometimes broke through the thick overcast to be followed by an earth-shaking roar. Suddenly the whole hillside seemed caught up in a fury of flames and thunderous sound. Now, thoroughly frightened, he crouched down as far as he could behind a rotted tree stump. The lad was Gleaves C. Beard, Sr., and child-like, he did not realize the danger. Later, when searchers found him still crouched in his tree-stump hide-away and questioned why he had left the house, he explained that he had 'wanted to see the firin (firing). When the battle was over in the late afternoon, Belmont showed the stark evidence of the day's battle. The tall white columns of pie-shaped brick were now scarred and shell-pocked. The weatherboarding was notched with bullet holes, and many windows were nicked and broken. The house was soon overrun by federal troops. One man, determined to be the first to gain entrance to the cellar, hoping to find the family's food supply, quickly sawed a hole through the floor. He dropped down into the darkness and into a barrel of soft soap. Years later, he stopped at the Beards' and recalled the incident." For information on the June 5, 1864, Battle of Piedmont, see *Conquest of a Valley* by Marshall M. Brice (McClure Printing Co., Verona, Va., 1960).

Suffice it to say that Belmont was in the midst of the action. The federals under General David Hunter attacked the position of General W. E. "Grumble" Jones, located not far northwest of Belmont, on the northern fringe of a heavily-wooded area. Jones and many of his men were killed in this engagement. Confederate General John Crawford Vaughn's Tennessee mounted infantry positioned its left flank just behind Belmont, extending to the east, with General John D. Imboden's reserves extending further to the east. General Vaughn's troops also suffered severe casualties.

Artillery was used heavily by both sides and whole segments of woods were entirely denuded of leaves and branches after the fierce cannonades. Brice mentions the Beard home frequently in his account. Following are two instances: "A hospital had been improvised during the battle and was now formally established in a farmhouse a mile from the battlefield. Other dwellings took in a few patients, including the Shaver House (north of the battlefield, where General Hunter had set up his first headquarters), the two Walker homes, the Beard House, and the McCue house across (west of) Middle River. . . . Several houses of the battlefield remain – the Beard House and the Shaver house, both almost unchanged in the hundred years."

The Howdyshells have a fine collection of artifacts from the Piedmont battlefield and a great many stories about the Beard family and its activities throughout the many generations they have resided at Belmont.

Note: Belmont also has several outbuildings to include a springhouse and a kitchen/washhouse. The two-level, rectangular brick springhouse has a gable entry with an overhang, a plastered ceiling, a brick floor, and storage above. The springhouse also has an ice house on one end that drains into the sunken springhouse trough. The kitchen/washhouse is a two-storied rectangular building with two bays (one per floor), a gable entry and gable roof, an external brick and stone chimney, and narrow beaded board paneling.

SOURCE: Joe Nutt, *Daily News Leader*, September 22, 1993.

Village Beginnings

Commercial buildings played an important role in the economic development of Augusta County since its early settlement. By the 1740s, specialized resident merchants had developed in the larger Valley towns such as Staunton. Before the Revolutionary War, stores were most commonly found in one or two remodeled rooms of the storekeeper's house; only in Staunton or Winchester did stores begin to assume a detached building form or become the main part of the house. According to Robert Mitchell, the eighteenth-century country store performed three major functions: "It was generally the only source of goods from the outside world, it operated as a market for local farm surplus, and it functioned as the most reliable source of credit. Eighteenth-century storekeepers were generally involved with farming as well, dividing their attentions between these two occupations."

Before the Revolution, there were still very few of these more isolated stores in the county. Often, peddlers served the same function by traveling around the countryside to the individual farms. However, in the late eighteenth and early nineteenth centuries, with the development of country towns, more stores were established in the county. By 1800, there were twenty-seven merchants in the Staunton and Augusta County area. These stores met the local demand for salt, sugar, cloth, powder, shot, shoes, knives, forks, liquor, and sundries. Most of the other products needed in the home were produced on the farm.

With the creation of more towns in Augusta County in the first half of the nineteenth century, an increasing number of stores were established in these villages. Often when a storekeeper began a store out in the country, several houses were soon clustered around the store, and a small community developed. The country store became the focus of many small towns and often served as a polling place and as a post office before rural mail delivery came into the county in the early twentieth century. As post offices were created across the county, they were commonly placed within one of these stores, usually still located in a house. Only a few detached store buildings were actually built during these years. During the antebellum years, other types of commercial enterprises such as taverns, small shops, and offices were increasingly built in these small towns, adding to their importance as commercial centers for the

surrounding countryside. By 1810, tanning and distilling also developed as major local industries. Tanneries produced large amounts of footwear and saddlery. In distilling, Augusta County was the leading producer in the state. The late twentieth century brought more years of prosperity to the county, and local towns flourished with a variety of commercial enterprises. During these years, local stores often evolved into the detached building form known today, and they expanded the variety of goods they sold. More shops were also created to meet the ever-increasing demand from the countryside. By the late nineteenth century and first decade of the twentieth century, many of the larger towns had established banks, reflecting the desire for specialization occurring by the turn of the century. Often, individual stores began to specialize in certain goods, since many towns generally had several stores.
SOURCE: With minor modification, the material above comes directly from Ann McCleary, Historic Resources in Augusta County, Va., "Eighteenth Century to the Present, Historic Landmarks of Virginia" (now Department of Historic Resources), 1982.

Stout-Fretwell-Garber General Merchandise Store Site

The country store often served several commercial functions to include post office, polling place, and community gathering spot. In rural communities, local men would sit by the stove, share local news, discuss politics, and

The New Hope General Merchandise Store was built in 1804. This photograph, taken in 1954, shows the addition on the left which was added sometime after 1907.

socialize. Women also found the country store to be a social outlet and a market for their goods such as milk, butter, eggs, and chickens. The assortment of goods sold by country stores constantly changed with the times as they moved from rooms in houses to larger, detached buildings. As more types of foodstuffs became readily available with advancements in the food industry, storekeepers would add these to their shelves. Many stores expanded into other goods, including ready-to-wear clothing, which became popular during the late nineteenth century.

By 1800, the New Hope area was beginning to get a network of dirt roads. It had numerous farms and houses and a couple of churches outside of the area but no stores. The area was poised for commercial development to support the farm economy and the needs of area farm residents. In the early nineteenth century, New Hope began its existence with the building of a general merchandise store. In 1804, James M. Stout built a rectangular, gable entry, three-bay, two-story brick building with a gable roof, hound's-tooth cornice, basement, main floor, and second floor. After 1907, a storage area with basement constructed of block was added to the left side of the building.

The New Hope General Merchandise Store sold meats, canned food, butter, eggs, clothes, horseshoe nails, kerosene, harness leather, and buggy grease. It has been reported that before the Civil War slaves were sold in front of the store. Prior to 1900, a pair of cattle scales adjoined the store property and was used to weigh the cattle that were purchased for slaughter on Fridays and sold as meat products that weekend.

In 1939, the store was called "H. F. Garber & Son, (Paul W. Garber) General Merchandise - Notions and Groceries, Fresh and Cured Meats a Specialty," and they sold canned goods, work clothes, needles and thread, salted fish, meats and cheese, ice and ice cream, candy and soft drinks, homemade sandwiches, gasoline and kerosene. Due to World War II, many things were in short supply, so Homer and Paul went to Richmond and bought used tires with bald spots and resold them to customers who commuted to Waynesboro to work. They butchered five beeves a week and sold the meat. Due to gasoline rationing, they were able to sell all the gasoline they could get. The store maintained a credit ledger and suffered no bad debts because everyone paid their bill when they were able. In 1951, the store was sold for $11,000 to C. William Garber and was sold to Nelson G. Hinebaugh about 1957. Then the store passed through several owner operators until it went out of business about 1975, due to competition from self-service super markets. Although the New Hope General Merchandise Store was one of the oldest brick structures in Augusta County, it was bulldozed in 1980 by Jefferson National Bank to make more parking available for the bank.

Known proprietors include:

Date	Proprietors
1804 to c1847	James M. Stout
1847 to c1860	Thornton G. Stout (b.12-4-1816, d.4-22-1904)
1860 to May 30, 1925	Franklin Fretwell & Son (William "Billy" Fretwell)
June 1, 1925 to July 1, 1939	Everett M. Garber
July 1, 1939 to June 30 1951	Homer F. Garber & Son (Paul W. Garber)
July 1, 1951 to 1957	C. William Garber
1957 to 1960	Nelson G. Hinebaugh
1961 to 1966	James W. Grove
1966 to 1968	Russell Shank
Closed c1975	Carl Caricofe

Note: After sitting empty for several years, it was bought by A. C. Lawhorne and Lester Anderson and used as an antique shop.

Dickerson-Fretwell Tavern

In the eighteenth century, taverns were some of the earliest commercial ventures to be established in the Valley. They served travelers coming through the area and were located along major thoroughfares and in villages and major towns. They also served as social centers for local people to gather and as post offices and polling places. Improved transportation and the development of roads and turnpikes in the early nineteenth century further encouraged the growth of taverns. Travelers often noted that taverns were located about every five or six miles to support stagecoach travel. Also, the popular distillery trade in the Valley helped support taverns by supplying whiskey, brandy, and beer to ordinaries throughout Augusta County. Most taverns were located in individual homes and followed the two-room, hall-parlor plan which was often enlarged by a lateral extension. They were generally long buildings, usually single-pile in depth and some had a two-story piazza across the front.

Around 1818, New Hope's second known public building was built and sits at the northeast corner of Routes 608 and 616. The business was started around 1818 to 1820 and was called the Dickerson Tavern in an 1847 deed from Dickerson to R. W. Dickerson. About 1852, it was sold to a William Frank Fretwell and continued as a tavern and stagecoach stop, which provided lodging, food, and rest for guests. The building was used as a hospital for Confederate soldiers in June of 1864 after the Battle of Piedmont. The Dickerson-Fretwell tavern has an outbuilding that was used as a kitchen. The one-story, one-bay building has a side entry with gable roof and external brick chimney flue.

Dickerson-Fretwell Tavern, built circa 1818

Postal Operations

Until 1829, a horse and rider carried the mail up the Valley Pike (Route 11) from Winchester to Staunton. Until 1826, mail for New Hope area residents was dropped off at the old Plow and Harrow Tavern in Mount Sidney near the intersection of the Keezletown Road with the Valley Pike and later the Mount Sidney Post Office. The New Hope postal operations were established on March 3, 1829, and were probably located in the New Hope General Merchandise Store where the post office is known to have operated for at least seventy-five years of its existence. Postal operations were a very important development in the evolution of New Hope.

New Hope Post Office, circa 1874

New Hope Mailman, circa 1905

It is not known precisely when rural mail delivery started in the New Hope area, but it was in the very early twentieth century.

After being located in a side room of Postmaster Marion Spitzer's house for twenty-five years, the New Hope Post Office moved into its own building specially designed for this purpose. The old post office was officially closed at 12:30 p.m. Saturday and the new facility opened its doors on Monday morning August 1, 1965. The completed brick masonry structure cost about $10,000 and contains nearly 900 square feet of floor space plus an outside loading platform.

Over the past 175 years, the New Hope Post Office has had the following postmasters:

Appointment	Postmaster	Location
March 3, 1829	Benjamin F. Frye	Unknown
December 29, 1836	William R. Stuart	Unknown
July 11, 1838	James M. Stout	Brick store
September 21, 1847	Thornton G. Stout	Brick store
October 12, 1865	Absolum D. Cullen	Unknown
December 14, 1871	Henry Myers	Unknown
August 4, 1874	Zack T. Kerr	Nelia Ray lot, south end of village
May 27, 1893	Mrs. Isabella Kerr	Nelia Ray lot, south end of village
September 25, 1896	Isabelle Kerr Swink	Nelia Ray lot, south end of village
April 20, 1897	Charles R. Parr	S.W. corner of Rs. 608 and 616
February 26, 1908	Benjamin Michael	Brick store
June 1, 1925	Everett M. Garber	Brick store
July 1, 1939	Walter N. Scrogham	Store across from New Hope School
February 1, 1940	Marion R. Spitzer	Spitzer home
August 1, 1965	Post office moved to a new brick building (present site).	
April 1, 1966	L. Beard	Brick Post Office Building
January 1, 1967	J. E. Grove	Brick Post Office Building
April 7, 1973	Billie T. Rosen	Brick Post Office Building
1997 - 1999	Barbara Baldwin	Brick Post Office Building
1999 - 2004	Robert Plum	Brick Post Office Building
January 8, 2005	Michael Chittum	Brick Post Office Building

The current brick post office in New Hope was built in 1965.

A Village Is Born

It is believed that by 1790 a few houses or log cabins existed along New Hope Road (present-day Route 608). However, the evolution of New Hope sprang from the building of a general store in 1804 and the Dickerson Tavern in 1818 as well as the commencement of postal operations in 1829. This spurred further community and commercial developments such as the building of churches, family farmsteads, grist mills, and additional houses. Some of those buildings still exist today.

Area Churches

The early religious history of Augusta County reflects the ethnic roots of its settlers. The Scotch-Irish, the first immigrants into the county in the 1730s and 1740s, established several Presbyterian churches throughout the county by 1800. Augusta Stone Church was built as early as 1740, followed soon after by Tinkling Spring Church. After the Revolutionary War, a wave of German migration brought several other denominations into the county in the 1780s and 1790s. The Lutherans and German Reformed often built churches together, worshipping at separate times. As their congregations grew, they eventually split and built their own churches. German Baptists also came and were called Tunkers or Dunkards and more recently the Church of the Brethren. The German Baptist became the largest German church in Augusta County in the nineteenth and twentieth centuries.

In the early nineteenth century, the lively, evangelical preaching of the Methodists and Baptists began to challenge these more established churches. Many Methodist and six Baptist churches were built among the white population by the end of the century. The United Brethren Church brought evangelical theology similar to the Methodists to the German settlers in the nineteenth century and became very popular by the late nineteenth century. The religious fervor of the Methodists and Baptists appealed to blacks as well. By proselytizing in the black communities, leaders of these churches contributed to the construction of numerous chapels and churches for black members throughout the county. All of the black churches built before the 1880s were aligned with either the Methodists or Baptists.

New Hope churches contributed greatly to the early development of the area. Records have been found that show active religious movement and church life in the New Hope vicinity before 1809. The Round Hill Meeting House was erected before March 17, 1809, and then the old *German Letter* called it the Eagle Church in 1809. It was used by two denominations to start with, Lutheran and Presbyterian Societies. The Methodists outgrew the others, and it was called the Providence Meeting House. The second church building was erected in 1850 and was a frame structure where the present United Methodist Church stands. George Peters and John Webb of Mt. Sidney, Virginia, erected the 1850 church structure for $950. It also served as a hospital for Confederate soldiers during the Civil War. The original church building was struck by a small cannon ball during the Battle of Piedmont.

In 1824, Abraham Garber was instrumental in building the first Dunker church in Augusta County and the second oldest Brethren Church in Virginia. It was a commodious brick building on a beautiful and convenient location on his farm and is known as the Middle River Church of the Brethren. The church house was used as a hospital during and after the Battle of Piedmont, which was fought in sight of the church. Some of the soldiers who died were buried in the church cemetery. Wooden markers were placed to mark the graves, but they have long since disappeared. The Middle River Church has the largest collection of nineteenth-century stones in the area with popular funerary motifs.
SOURCE: With minor modification, first two paragraphs come directly from Ann McCleary, Historic Resources in Augusta County, Va., "Eighteenth Century to the Present, Historic Landmarks of Virginia" (now Department of Historic Resources), 1982.

Augusta Stone Presbyterian Church (Old Stone), above, was built in the 1740s (photograph circa 1907), while Trinity Lutheran was founded in 1772, making it the oldest Lutheran congregation in Augusta County. The two represent the oldest churches in the New Hope area.

Middle River Church of the Brethren

In the early nineteenth century, very few church houses had been built by the Brethren in Virginia and buildings were needed. Dr. John S. Flory wrote about the church house built at Middle River and the story of this enterprise reads almost like a story out of legendary lore. In the summer of 1824, Abraham Garber led a group of workmen to the backside of his farm and set them to building a brick kiln. This finished, he set them to digging up the clay and preparing it for a large kiln. In a seemingly short time there was a stack of bricks sufficient for a large building. The next step was to set the men to work erecting the walls of the church under the direction of an experienced bricklayer. So efficiently was everything managed, it is said that before the snow began to fly the walls were up, the building roofed and furnished with hastily constructed benches, and the big fireplaces, one at each end, were ablaze with hickory wood from the forest. If this story, as it has come down to us, is not literally true in every detail, it is certainly true in its general purport, and is highly representative of the time and the spirit in which the Brethren went about establishing themselves and the church they loved. Before the end of 1824, the congregation was organized with Abraham Garber as the first elder. Dr. Flory wrote: "At the same time he presented to the congregation a will, which conveyed to them the church building along with the plot of ground on which it stood, all free of debt, as a freewill gift to the newly organized Brick Church Congregation of Augusta County, Virginia."

The first Middle River Church, founded by Abraham Garber in 1824. (From a 1970s artist's rendition of original church.)

The building of a new church was a signal to expand. An organizational meeting elected two young men to the ministry, John Garber and David Miller. Garber was the oldest son of Abraham, and Miller was the son of David Miller. These young men were installed as ministers, and prospects for the church were bright. The new church house and the addition of new ministers helped attract other settlers to Middle River. As sections of the counties farther north were more fully occupied, more of the newcomers went on southward into Augusta County. They found fertile soil along Middle River, which was well suited to the building of their homes.

The period from 1824 to 1850 was a period of growth and development for the Brick congregation on Middle River. The building of the house of worship was the second in the Valley and the first in Augusta County. The congregation had an able staff of officers headed by Abraham Garber, who led the work until his death in 1846 at the age of eighty-six. During this period, John Garber and Peter Miller were the other elders, and the ministers were Daniel Brower, Jacob Brower, and Martin Garber. The membership had increased to more than 500 members, and the Shenandoah Valley had become a leading center of Brethren influence. Middle River was the only congregation of the Brethren in Augusta County, but seven other congregations were in Shenandoah and Rockingham Counties.

During these years, the Annual Meeting of the then-German Baptist Brethren had been held from time to time in Pennsylvania, Maryland, Virginia, and Ohio. In 1851, it was held at the Brick Church on Middle River. With membership over 500, Middle River was one of the largest congregations in the Valley and its members were widely scattered. Meetings had been held in various homes and schoolhouses in different parts of the territory served by Middle

Middle River Church of the Brethren, second building built 1884, photograph 1905.

River. After careful consideration, the congregation reached a general agreement to build two new church houses. One was to be several miles north of the Brick Church and the other several miles south. After these two new churches were properly staffed, the territory would be divided into three congregations. The church to the north was Pleasant Valley; the one to the south was Barren Ridge. In 1854, when John Garber and Peter Miller died, the Pleasant Valley Church was under construction and was built and dedicated two years later. John Miller was ordained elder and placed in charge of the Pleasant Valley Church; John Brower was ordained and placed in charge at Barren Ridge.

When the congregation was divided, there were nine ministers at Middle River. Their allotment with that of the membership was determined by the congregation lines, which on the whole proved satisfactory. In these allotments the parent church, Middle River, had slightly more than 200 members with Martin Garber and Daniel Brower elders and John Brower, Levi Garber, and Daniel Yount as ministers. Pleasant Valley had around 150 members with John Miller as elder and Abram D. Garber as minister. Barren Ridge started with about 100 members. John Brower was elder with Enoch Brower as minister. It seems that these new congregations were officially started in 1865.

SOURCE: W. Paul Coffman, *A History of Middle River Congregation, Church of the Brethren,* 1964.

New Hope United Methodist Church

The beginnings of Methodism in the New Hope area are shrouded in uncertainty. The records of those earliest days, which would be so highly prized today, are non-existent. Undoubtedly the pattern was the same as that found elsewhere: small groups of believers meeting in homes and being visited at irregular intervals by the itinerant preachers who traveled in great hardship and privation from group to group, their circuits covering a county or counties in the early days.

The first church buildings in the New Hope area were Old Stone Presbyterian at Ft. Defiance (Augusta Stone), built around 1740, and Trinity Lutheran, established in 1772. The first house of worship in the New Hope community was the old log building known as the Round Hill Meeting House. This building was erected prior to 1809, when James Kerr and George Rutledge deeded one acre and ninety-five poles of land to George Barnhart and Balser Tevenbaugh, trustees for the Lutheran and Presbyterian Societies on March 27, 1809 (Augusta County Deed Book 35). This building was used by several denominations (German and English) as a school, meeting house, and burying ground. It seems that the Methodists grew faster and the name came to be associated with them. The subsequent Methodist houses of worship bore the name of Round Hill or Providence Meeting House.

New Hope United Methodist Church built 1850, photograph circa 1909

Just where this first church stood cannot be definitely determined on the basis of present information. We do know that it was the first of three houses of worship for this congregation. The second church was a frame building situated, most likely, on the present plot of the church property. In 1839, Edward Rutledge deeded a piece of ground which is a part of the present holdings to Zachariah Johnson, Charles Batis, Samuel Harnesbarger, and Samuel Kennerly, Trustees "that they shall keep the buildings now erected thereon, or some similar and convenient building for a meeting house, a place of public worship called the Round Hill or Providence Meeting House for the use of the members of the Methodist Church in U.S. of America." In 1849, a contract was given to George Peters by the Round Hill Congregation to build the present Methodist Church. This present building was erected in 1850 and dedicated in 1852. During and following the Battle of Piedmont in June 1864, this church was used as a hospital for Confederate soldiers wounded in the battle. A small projectile struck the church at this time, and the hole in the siding was shown to visitors until the church was remodeled in 1929.

During the latter days of the war, the church suffered great abuse. It is said that Union soldiers used to ride their horses in one door and out the other, there being two rear doors. At one time, an attempt was made to burn the church, though the burning of churches was not a practice of the Union Army, but the group was driven off by a patrol of Confederates who were stationed as observers on Round Hill.

Originally a high platform extended all the way across the front of the church, and the pulpit was reached by stairs. In 1869, this high platform was cut down somewhat in height and at the same time kerosene lamps were installed in holders fastened to the side walls. The first organ was bought in 1878. Miss Kate Weller and Miss Laura Eakle took turns playing the instrument. A few years later Mrs. Sadie Kerr became the regular organist. A great revival lasting six weeks occurred during the pastorate of Rev. G. T. D. Collins in the fall of 1867. The church was crowded to capacity, and there were many professions of faith. It was also about this time that a very successful choir was organized and the good music was a great attraction to the services.

New Hope United Methodist Church as it appeared before remodeling in 1929.

In 1919, there was considerable agitation for the building of a new church, and a committee did some work on the plans and preparation, but the project was deferred. In 1929, the building underwent a great deal of remodeling. A different entrance was provided by the addition of a vestibule and stairs and the construction of six Sunday school rooms, new floors, painting, and furnishings. Later Venetian blinds were put up and the oil heating plant installed in 1947. The first piano was a gift of Sam Bauserman after the death of his wife in 1933.

Pastors called:

John W. Start	1854-1856
Philip S. E. Sixeas	1856-1860
W. C. McCarty	1860-1861
William R. Stringer	1861-1863
Robert Smith	1863-1866
J. J. Engle	1866-1869
A. A. P. Neel	1869-1870
John W. Wolfe	1870-1873
John S. S. Hutchinson	1873-1874
Joshua M. Grandin	1874-1875
Joseph H. Temple	1875-1876
Lewis H. Graybill	1876-1878
Andrew Robey	1878-1879
Charles G. Linthicum	1879-1880
Addison Weller	1880-1882
Rufus H. Wilson	1882-1886
George T. D. Collins	1886-1888
Walter W. Watts	1888-1889
Thomas Briley	1889-1891
Charles L. Potter	1892-1893
Thomas J. Miller	1893-1895
Thomas Cooper	1895-1897
J. Kyle Gilbert	1897-1899
Asbury R. Martin	1899-1901
Oscar F. Burgess	1901-1904
C. B. Sutton	1904-1908
Wm. M. Compton	1908-1909
Frederick E. Allison	1909
George H. Echols	1919-1913
Vincent W. Wheeler	1913-1914
Clarence J. Clark	1914-1918
Linwood Hammond	1918-1920
Byron W. John	1920-1921
Hamilton M. Roane	1921
M. Conway Weikel	1921-1922
Edward Lee Wine	1922
George E. Pope	1923-1925
Benjamin Lee Parrott	1925-1927
John Calvin Thrasher	1927-1928
Harry L. Coffman	1928-1932
Julian Eugene White	1932-1934
George L. Waters	1934-1936
Robert O. Hipes	1936-1946
Harold E. Skelton	1946-1953
Arthur E. Shelton	1953-1956
Merrell H. Barton	1956-1958
Wm. S. Hopkins, Jr.	1959-1961
Albert N. Fritter	1961-1963
John E. Davis, Jr.	1963-1968
Howard C. Smith	1968-1979
Rudolph Benesh	1979-1983
Glen Evans	1983-1986
Clyde Weaver, Jr.	1986-1990
Steve Proctor	1990-1996
Fred Arndt	1993-1996
S. Wayne Rickman	1996-2001
Douglas Gunsalas	2001-Present

SOURCE: Taken from Nathaniel Barnhart, *United Methodist Church History, New Hope, Virginia, (1806-1972).*

Mt. Tabor Methodist Church

Churches usually form the focus of rural black communities, and Round Hill is no exception. The Mt. Tabor Methodist Church is located in the Round Hill community on Route 784 one mile southeast of New Hope, around Round Hill itself. This community developed in the late nineteenth century. Few blacks were there in 1885, but a "colored church" and school did exist. Today Round Hill is home to two black churches; the former "colored school" grew but was closed in 1961.

The Mt. Tabor Church with its cemetery is the oldest surviving black church in Augusta County. It was first called the Round Hill Providence Church. The congregation was established in 1841 by a few Christians who were interested in renewing their strength in Christ. The first church building was a v-notched log structure built in the 1870s. Richard K. MacMaster, in his book *Augusta*

County History, 1865-1950, states that the Freedman's Bureau contributed toward the construction of New Hope's Mt. Tabor Methodist Church. The log building is a traditional rectangular, gable entry form but is smaller and lower in elevation and completely unadorned. This is the only log church surviving in Augusta County. The log structure served its members for many years until a new white frame building was constructed in 1900. The log structure has been well maintained and serves as the church fellowship hall today.

SOURCE: Ann McCleary, Historic Resources in Augusta County, Va., "Eighteenth Century to the Present, Historic Landmarks of Virginia" (now Department of Historic Resources), 1982; Richard K. MacMaster, *Augusta County History, 1865-1950*; and discussions between church member Clairrine Veney and Owen Harner, spring 2005.

Mt. Tabor Methodist Church began in the log structure seen in the top photo. About 1900 the congregation constructed the frame church seen in front of the log building.

Mt. Bethel Baptist Church

The Mt. Bethel Baptist Church is an off-shoot of the Mt. Tabor Methodist Church. In 1900, a group of church members formed a Baptist congregation known as the Bethel Church. When this group of members broke from Mt. Tabor, they met in an old building near the location of the present church for a number of years before a new church building was erected. In 1930, the name was changed again to Mt. Bethel Church and later to Mt. Bethel Baptist Church. The congregation's motto is *"Small in Number but Large in Faith."*

Mt. Bethel Baptist Church, 1900–1918

In 2001, the Mt. Tabor Methodist Church and the Mt. Bethel Baptist Church celebrated their combined 133rd anniversary. During their combined history, the two congregations have called the following pastors:

Rev. N. P Hawkins (1870-1900)
Rev. Carr (1900-1909)
Rev. Wesley Jones (1909-1910)
Rev. F. W. Pennick (1911-1915)
Rev. A. L. Brent (1915-1924)
Rev. Mayo (1924-1926)
Rev. T. M. Johnson (1926-1929)
Rev. J. H. Taylor (1929-1932)
Rev. George W. Stewart (1932-1940)
Rev. C. H Harris (1940-1952)
Rev. Thomas Cary Allen (1952-1977)
Rev. Frederick H. Bagley (1977-1987
Rev. Diamond (1987-1992)
Rev. Milton Dandridge (1992-2000)
Rev. Willie Washington (2000-present)

SOURCE: Based on an unpublished congregational history as well as discussions between Clairrine Veney and Owen Harner.

New Hope Presbyterian Chapel

The New Hope Presbyterian Chapel was started by the Old Stone Presbyterian Church at Ft. Defiance. It is believed that the chapel was built in the early 1890s. Ruth McBride Gill, daughter of the late Rev. McBride who was pastor at Old Stone Church in the 1930s–40s, remembers coming to the New Hope Chapel with her father in the late 1930s. Services were held every other Sunday night until poor attendance caused the services to be discontinued in 1939. In 1942 (middle of WWII), newlyweds Paul and Ruby Garber bought the vacated New Hope Presbyterian Chapel and rebuilt it into a house. Because of the shortage of building materials, one could not obtain a permit to build a new residence, but they were given a permit to renovate. The Garbers occupied their new house in 1943, started a family, and lived there until 1952.

SOURCE: Interviews with Mrs. Mel Livick and Paul and Ruby Garber.

New Hope Presbyterian Chapel, built circa 1890, photograph taken about 1907.

New Hope Presbyterian Chapel, photograph circa 1940.

Church Cemeteries

Middle River Cemetery

Location: The cemetery is located at the Middle River Church of the Brethren, which is two miles northwest of New Hope, Virginia, Augusta County on Route 778.

Summary Assessment: This is a well-kept cemetery and has many interesting epitaphs. The earliest date is 1829 and some of the dates are written differently from any found elsewhere. One Civil War veteran killed at the Battle of Piedmont is buried here. There are several German names and names which were changed at various times from the original spelling.

Source: Library of Virginia Titled Files: Survey Report, Middle River Graveyard, August 12, 1936, research made by Scioto M. Herndon. This write-up is a part of the Virginia W.P.A. Historical Inventory Project sponsored by the Virginia Conservation Commission under the direction of its Division of History.

New Hope Cemetery

Location: The cemetery is located at the New Hope United Methodist Church, which is south of New Hope, Virginia, Augusta County, near the intersection of Routes 608 and 617

Summary Assessment: This cemetery is on a sloping hillside and is well kept. There are no fallen stones and none of the graves have sunken very far. There are a number of wooden and rock markers which bear no inscriptions. The earliest date is 1850. There are very few old epitaphs in the cemetery. The grave of Wm. A. Mauser, killed in the Battle of Piedmont, July 6, 1864, is here.

Source: Library of Virginia Titled Files: Survey Report, New Hope Graveyard, August 12, 1936, research made by Scioto M. Herndon. This write-up is a part of the Virginia W.P.A. Historical Inventory Project sponsored by the Virginia Conservation Commission under the direction of its Division of History.

Mt. Tabor Cemetery

Location: The cemetery is located at the Mt. Tabor United Methodist Church, which is one mile east of New Hope, Virginia, Augusta County, on Route 617, Round Hill School Road.

Summary Assessment: The church's cemetery has unmarked and marked graves. Some graves are marked with yuccas (plants). Other graves are marked with plain or uncarved stones, hand carved, and mass produced stones of the twentieth century.

Yucca plant

Mt. Bethel Cemetery

Location: The cemetery is located at the

Mt. Bethel Baptist Church, which is one mile east of New Hope, Virginia, Augusta County, on Route 617, Round Hill School Road.
Summary Assessment: The church cemetery has unmarked graves with yuccas (plants) as markers and a few mass-produced stones.

Private Graveyards

Eakle Graveyard

Location: The family graveyard is located one-quarter mile southwest of Cross Roads Service Station, just above New Hope, Virginia, Augusta County.
Summary Assessment: This graveyard is located in a field and surrounded by cedar trees and rocks. It has not been maintained and is almost unrecognizable as a graveyard.

Humbert Graveyard

Location: This graveyard is located on the Garber farm, about a half mile west of New Hope, Virginia, Augusta County, and is reached by a side road and a lane. This graveyard is situated on the top of a low rise and surrounded by wheat and cornfields. There is a thick growth of aspens and a hedge around it. The trees are very close together; it was necessary to crawl under them to reach the stones.
Summary Assessment: This is one of the most interesting of the private plots, and the stones must have been very beautiful at one time. There is carving of roses and cypress trees and much scroll work. The spelling is interesting and some of the letters are reversed. Many of the inscriptions are hand-scratched with some sharp instrument and are not quite plumb. The earliest date is 1799 and the latest is 1857. Some stones are broken and a few cannot be read. The stones have scattered and some are piled at one side so they do not rest above the graves they cover. The ground is uneven; there are many holes which may have been made by groundhogs. This plot, now owned by the Garbers, was obtained by an early grant and originally owned by the Humbert family. It is believed that the original owner is buried here, but, if so, the stone has disappeared. In 2005, the authors visited the site and found it to be unrecognizable as a graveyard. Raspberry vines and groundhog holes were prevalent, trash and debris covered the site, and the remains of an old building had been deposited on the site.
Source: Library of Virginia Titled Files: Survey Report, Humbert Graveyard, August 12, 1936, research made by Scioto M. Herndon. This write-up is a part of the Virginia W.P.A. Historical Inventory Project sponsored by the Virginia Conservation Commission under the direction of its Division of History.

McCullogh Graveyard

Location: This small family graveyard is located in a clump of trees on Humbert Road 200 yards from Route 608 and behind the Showalter-Early House. This graveyard was visited by Wayne Garber and Owen Harner, April 14, 2005.
Summary Assessment: The boundaries of the graveyard are not marked and the carved headstones are in disarray.

Old Myers Graveyard

Location: This family graveyard on the Joseph L. Early farm is located just west of New Hope, Virginia. This graveyard was visited by Wayne Garber and Owen Harner, April 14, 2005.

Summary Assessment: This graveyard is surrounded by a rusted iron fence that is falling down, and many of the well-carved stones are broken or covered with dirt from groundhog holes.

Myers Graveyard

Location: This family graveyard plot is located on the south end of New Hope behind the Myers-Eutsler house. This graveyard was visited by Wayne Garber and Owen Harner, March 18, 2005.

Summary Assessment: This small family plot is not fenced off and the three beautifully carved headstones are in disarray and covered with briars.

Family Farmsteads

New Hope is located in the Middle River District, which contains some of the best farmland in Augusta County as both Middle River and South River wind through it. Farms have been the foundation of New Hope's development since the eighteenth century and most of the area surrounding New Hope today is engaged in farming. Farms needed a community support system; thus New Hope evolved to support the area's farm economy and became part of the Valley's system of town-centered settlements in the nineteenth century.

The family farm is composed of two major components; the domestic yard with the main house as its centerpiece and the farmyard with the barn as its main focus. Almost all of the surviving barns in the New Hope area are of frame construction and date to the post-Civil War period. Extensive barn burning during the Civil War, as well as other farm fires, brought the destruction of many early barns. The bank barn is clearly the most common barn form in the area and examples date from the mid-nineteenth century to the 1930s. This distinctive two-level design contains the hay mows with thrashing floor and granaries on the upper or main level, accessible by a ramp from the uphill side. Cattle stalls are located in the lower, banked level, with entry provided at grade level on the other side. A characteristic overhang or forebay extends along the side opposite the ramp, sheltering the row of doors to the lower-level cattle stalls and providing much-needed ventilation. Heavy mortise and tendon framing was used in most bank barns. In the late nineteenth century, circle sawn timbers replaced the early hewn and vertical sawn members. Foundations were almost always constructed of stone, and gable roofs appeared on most bank barns.

A southern view of New Hope farmland

SOURCE: With minor modification, the previous paragraph comes directly from Ann McCleary, Historic Resources in Augusta County, Va., "Eighteenth Century to the Present, Historic Landmarks of Virginia" (Department of Historic Resources), 1982.

Willberger Farmstead

The Willberger Farm from the late nineteenth century is pictured at right with its house, barn, and funeral home. The buildings are painted gray with white trim, which is somewhat unusual. The picture was taken before New Hope Road was paved in 1912.

Willberger farm, built circa 1890, photo about 1910

Mowry Farmstead

A steam tractor pulls an early hay baler. Photograph taken about 1905 in front of the Mowry bank barn near Piedmont.

A steam engine tractor powers a belt grinder about 1905 in front of the Mowry bank barn near Piedmont.

Typical of the type of horse-drawn transportation vehicles seen in New Hope in the late nineteenth and early twentieth centuries are these two from the Mowry farm. A farm wagon pulled by a team of work horses is seen in the top image, while a horse and sled are seen in the bottom photograph. Both photos were taken around 1905.

Bank Barns

***Fretwell barn**, built circa 1870–This red barn, once located in the heart of New Hope across from the New Hope Post Office, represents a typical frame bank barn in the area. Traditionally, painters used a combination of white on red or green on white. This picture was taken in May 1991. The barn was torn down about 2000.*

***Roberts-Obenschain barn**, built 1870–Bank barn built by Dr. William Roberts as part of the Roberts-Obenschain farmstead. Photograph taken in 2005 before the barn was torn down in June of 2005.*

***Willberger bank barn**, built circa 1880–This bank barn originally had an oak shake roof and is located behind the Dickerson-Fretwell Tavern. The straw shed was added about 1920 when disease struck the pine trees in the area. This picture was taken in 2005.*

Some farms have many different types of common outbuildings such as granaries, chicken houses, pig pens, corncribs, sheds, and dairy barns.

The chicken house, 1930

Swine were an important element on an Augusta County farm. The pig pen at left dates to 1982, while the two hog butchering scenes date to about 1930. Note the various sheds seen in the background of the top butchering scene.

Farm Work

Life on the farm was labor intensive.

Plowing was a time-consuming farm chore. Minor Garber, top photo above, plows his fields about 1905, while the team below is plowing in 1910.

Four generations of Garbers turned out to the fields in 1913 to make hay. In 1922, the Garber family was captured in this image as they hauled hay from the field.

In 1916, Lizzie Garber's chores included weeding the garden and feeding the animals.

Hauling wood, circa 1920

New Hope's windmill for pumping water, photograph taken in 1978

Dairy Farming

The popularity of large-scale dairy farming from the 1920s to the present led to the construction of modern dairy barns and silos to meet the improved standards for sanitation required on dairy farms. The Myers-Early farm was one of the first Grade-A dairy farms in the New Hope area. The dairy operation started in 1956 with a three-stall barn and expanded to a six-stall herringbone barn in 1972. The farm's 272 acres (original tract 112 acres) were located between Routes 617 and 608 and supported 250 to 300 head of dairy cattle. Hay, corn, and wheat were raised on the farm to support the dairy operation. The farm has good sources of water to include a never-failing spring and an ever-flowing creek.

Past farm owners include David and Elizabeth Myers, Isaac S. Myers and family, Elder Abraham B. Early, Joseph Myers Early, and Joseph Leonard Early. The present owner is Kenneth Showalter. The L-shaped farm house was originally built about 1890 and remodeled to a square house with hip roof in 1927. A living room and columns were added in 1957. About 1900 the A-frame bank barn was

built of oak timbers cut from Round Hill. The straw shed was added in the early 1930s. The picture below shows the original dairy milking parlor (bottom left with green roof), white frame house, and red barn.
SOURCE: Interview with Joseph Leonard Early by Wayne Garber in 2005.

Myers-Early dairy farm, circa 1958

Grist Mill Sites

Grist mills were one of the first industries to develop in eighteenth-century Augusta County. The earliest mills were usually located along large rivers and near major roads. The presence of gristmills often stimulated the development of secondary county roads and sometimes small communities developed around these mills. The cultivation of wheat as a major agricultural crop encouraged the establishment of gristmills. Local mills generally fell into two categories – custom mills or merchant mills. The non-commercial custom mills did custom grinding for individual farmers, charging a percentage of the total grain ground. In contrast, commercial or merchant mills bought grain from farmers, ground it, and marketed the flour. Traditionally, merchant mills ground mainly wheat, while custom mills also ground corn and other grains for farm use. The number of gristmills continued to grow throughout the nineteenth century. By 1879, a federal census recorded fifty-four grist and flouring mills, and the Hotchkiss

maps of 1884 showed eighty-one mills. These gristmills often had a sawmill at the same site, which served wood-using industries. The importance of wheat in the local economy led to the beginnings of dairy, cattle, and poultry farming, which became more important and widespread than wheat.
SOURCE: With minor modification, the material above comes directly from Ann McCleary, Historic Resources in Augusta County, Va., "Eighteenth Century to the Present, Historic Landmarks of Virginia" (now Department of Historic Resources), 1982.

Because of poor roads before 1900 and because of the fall of Middle, North and South Rivers and Naked Creek and the volume of water in these streams, numerous mills utilizing waterpower were erected along them in northeastern Augusta County. These mills were so close together that a local farmer did not have to travel more than five miles to reach a mill. These mills were places where farmers had their wheat ground into flour, bran, and shorts and their corn into cornmeal; where they could learn the prices at which grains and livestock were selling; where they could discuss religion and politics; and where they could gossip about local comedies and tragedies. The local miller was usually a knowledgeable and interesting personality.

In 1803, James Kerr built the first known saw and gristmill on Middle River. His sawmill was constructed of wood and measured forty feet by sixteen feet. The gristmill was a thirty-foot by thirty-foot two-story building with the first story constructed of stone and the second story of wood. In 1805, he built a second thirty-by-thirty gristmill, with one story of stone and two stories of wood, and a second sawmill, forty-by-sixteen feet, near the first gristmill.

Garber-Sites-Drumheller Mill

The old Garber-Sites-Drumheller Mill, known to be more than 150 years old, is being dismantled [in 1975] by a Charlottesville crew and will become part of the Michie Tavern complex on VA 53, near Monticello. The four-story, historic mill building which was once used to treat Civil War soldiers before they were transferred to the make-shift hospital at Middle River Church of the Brethren, north of here, will be made into a one-and-a-half-story structure. The remains of the old mill stand beside VA 907 or what once was VA 612 on Meadow Run. At one time, a blacksmith shop stood near the mill, but the late John F. Drumheller never used it. What he did use was the grist or flourmill, cider mill and sawmill. In fact, his son, Carson M. Drumheller, and his wife Charlotte operated the cider and sawmill and ground cornmeal and feed and cleaned wheat for local farmers until 1958. They bought the Drumheller home place in 1935. John Drumheller last made a brand of flour known as White Rose in 1933.

Garber-Sites-Drumheller Mill, built circa 1820. The wheel had already been removed for transport to Charlottesville when this photograph was taken.

Sitting on his back porch, Mr. Drumheller recalled the days when he helped his father deliver flour by horse and wagon to local stores and to Staunton and Waynesboro. He also remembers his father sleeping in the mill on a cot when he ground flour by waterpower. The dam that fed water to the mill was converted from logs to concrete in 1916. Carson Drumheller bought a power unit for the sawmill after he took over the operation. Although his wife was his main standby, his son, Carson, Jr., also helped on the mills. Mr. Drumheller retired from guard duty at American Safety Razor Co. about 18 months ago, and his wife retired about a year ago from the same plant [written in 1975}.

He sold the mill building to Joseph Conte, owner and operator of the historic Michie Tavern property. It will still be called Drumheller's Mill. Michie Tavern was built by Patrick Henry's father, Major John Henry, in 1735. Each of the four floors in Drumheller's Mill was supported by two 46-foot long hand-hewn beams. Wooden pegs and cut nails were used and are being saved for the reconstruction project. Mr. Conte said he plans to restore the burr grinder, the water wheel, and corn sheller. Blind persons will use a portion of the building as a craft shop.

It is believed that Abraham Garber built the mill prior to 1821, when the first deed mentioning it was recorded. Mr. Garber and his wife Barbara deeded it to Jacob Mohler on October 1, 1821. The Mohlers sold the property to David Myers on April 5, 1848, and he, in turn, deeded it to Christian Myers on August 8, 1851. Christian and Catharine Myers sold the grist and sawmills to Silas

Korner on September 1, 1854. The Korners deeded the mill and water rights to John Schutterlee on August 31, 1855. The Schutterlees sold the mill property, which consisted of fifty acres, for $6,000 to Windle Sites. The right was given Mr. Windle Sites to raise the mill dam, "the mark being an auger hole made in a rock on the opposite or southeast side of the dam a few feet above the abutment on Long Meadow Run." Mr. Sites, who owned the mill during the Civil War years, was a member of the German Baptist Brethren Church (Church of the Brethren today), or Dunkards as they were often nicknamed. This Christian sect believed in nonresistance and peace. Therefore, Mr. Sites did not take part in the war. It is told that when Union troops passed through the area in the late days of the war, they respected his convictions and non-participation in the war and the beliefs of his church and spared his mill from fire.

Census records of 1860 show that the mill was valued at $6,000 and was run by waterpower. One male was employed at $24 a month, and the mill used 3,000 bushels of wheat valued at $4,000 and 3,000 bushels of corn and rye. Three hundred barrels of flour were valued at $5,000 and 3,000 barrels of meal were being ground per month. Ten years later, the census declared the mill to be worth $5,000. Rated at 15 horsepower, it was still run by water. Hiring one man, it had two burrs and operated on a nine-month basis. Production was listed as 6,000 bushels of wheat at $6,000, 500 bushels of rye at $500, 200 bushels of corn at $200, and 1,320 barrels of flour at $6,600. Windle and Meary Sites sold the mill property to Silvester G. Stover on October 22, 1888, and he sold it to Fred and Joseph Frey on December 4, 1890. The Freys sold it to John Drumheller for $700 on December 12, 1896.
SOURCE: Roy Stephenson "Ancient Mill Moved to Michie Tavern," *Staunton News Leader*, circa 1975.

Windle Sites Tilt-Hammer Mill

A short distance down the Meadow Run from the Garber-Sites-Drumheller Mill is a natural stone waterfall. On a level plot just below this small waterfall is the site of Windle Sites' tilt-hammer mill. There was a blacksmith shop adjacent to the grist/sawmill, and the tilt-hammer mill, run by water power, was probably used in conjunction with this shop to forge nails. Will Sites has samples of the different sizes of nails beat out by the tilt-hammer mill. They all have rectangular, nearly square heads, and rectangular shanks taping to a blunt "point" end. They are of iron and unevenly formed, but well made.

The tilt-hammer was washed out in a bad flood in 1871 or 1872, Sites said, and only family anecdotes and a few surviving nails remain to recall its existence. Sites said that, apparently, the water wheel operated a mechanism that lifted (pulled) the hammer up and then released it to beat out the nails, which were probably heated to some malleable stage. Sites said his father used to find nails downstream for years after the mill was washed out.

The little stone waterfall impounds a fair-sized pond that provided a good iceskating rink in winter. The little rivulets over and around the stone falls provided a good spot for handsnaring stream suckers, up to two pounds in size, in spring.

SOURCE: Joe Nutt, "More on Mills: Tilt-Hammer and Others," *Staunton News Leader*, September 1992.

Humbert-Knightly Mill

One of the two most significant mills on Middle River was the Humbert-Knightly Mill, located on Route 778 where the road crosses Middle River. According to C. E. May, the Humbert-Knightly was known first as Allison Mill, next as Humbert's Mill, then as Hope Mill, and finally as Knightly Mill. This mill was established on a small grant of land to Robert Wiley and a tract of land Jacob Fisher acquired through several purchases. Jacob and David Humbert purchased, on May 10, 1819, a mill seat on Middle River with the right to raise the mill dam to such a height as might be necessary. The mill dam was built before July 27, 1833, per an agreement between Daniel and Jacob Humbert and William Allison. The Humbert Merchant Mill and sawmill situated on a seven-acre tract of land on Middle River was conveyed to Samuel Garber on January 22, 1853. Four years later, it became known as the Hope Mill when a half interest was conveyed by William Beard to David Beard. Over the next fifty years, either a full or partial interest in the mill was conveyed many times to the following people: Mansfield Marshall, Harrison Ross, David Myers, Christian Cline, Joseph Cline, John Wampler, D. A. Garber, John M. Cline, D. Baxter Lucas, Joseph Norford, Daniel S. Garber, and Minor Garber.

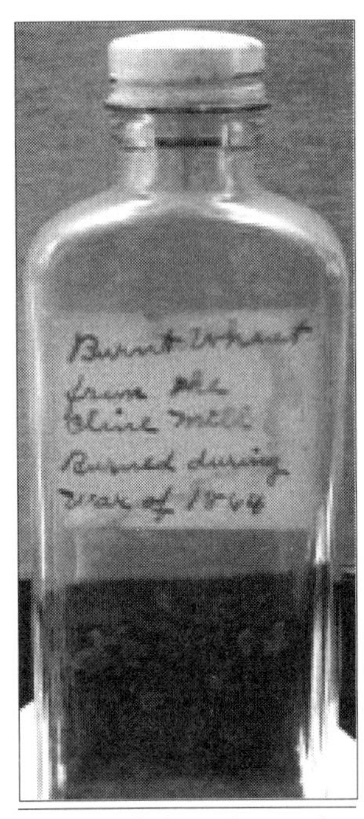

Some of the wheat that burned in the fall of 1864 when Union soldiers destroyed the Humbert-Knightly Mill has remained in the Garber family as a reminder of Civil War tragedies.

In 1864, the original mill building was burned by Civil War General Philip Sheridan's northern soldiers during the Valley's scorched earth campaign. It was rebuilt after the war as a three-story rectangular building with the top story lighted by a dormer with gable roof.

During the period 1870 to 1873, the

Original Humbert-Knightly Mill, built 1830s, photo taken in 1864 before it was rebuilt following its destruction in the Civil War.

Humbert-Knightly Mill was owned by Christian Cline, a farmer and miller. He was also the first treasurer of the East Augusta Mutual Fire Insurance Company. On June 16, 1870, Christian Cline contracted the following policies:

#33 Wooden building 50 x 20 ft., 2 stories, with porch and kitchen 18 x 24 ft.; valued $825, insured $550.

#34 Swisher barn 72 x 54 ft., with granary and stables; valued $825, insured $550.

In addition, the following policies are recorded in the name of Mrs. Rebecca Cline and Co.:

#399 Mill house on Middle River 36 x 50 ft., 5 stories with counting room and sawmill attached; valued $3,000, insured $1,500.

#433 Frame miller's house 12 x 15 ft., 2 stories, with two stone chim neys, new; valued $300, insured $200.

The Humbert-Knightly Mill was conveyed to Daniel S. Garber and Joseph Norford on May 31, 1905, for $6,500. Daniel Garber operated the mill from 1905 to 1912 and the facility consisted of a dam on Middle River, a millrace, a five-story frame mill house with two waterwheels, a wheat elevator, a sawmill, water rights, miller's house, and a flour warehouse situated on land of Valley Railroad Company near the Ft. Defiance Depot. The dam was originally made of logs and then was rebuilt of concrete about 1920 by a Mr. Harris from

Rebuilt Humbert-Knightly Mill, photograph taken in the 1870s. Note the wagons full of wheat awaiting unloading.

Charlottesville. The mill ground wheat for local farmers and bought wheat from farmers to grind and resell. Daniel employed his son, Minor Garber, who worked in the flour mill and sawmill in the wintertime. Daniel kept black snakes in the mill for mouse control, which proved to be very effective. The products sold were white flour and whole flour that were labeled "White Lilly," and the tag line on the flour sacks was "None Better." Many people in the area made clothing from the flour sacks.

On July 1, 1912, Daniel sold a half interest in the mill to his son for $4,000 because he did not like the dust associated with the milling business. The half interest included the land, the water rights, the dam rights, the miller's house, and the flour warehouse on the land of the Valley Railroad near Ft. Defiance Depot. About 1916, Minor Garber installed two dynamos in the mill to generate electricity and build an electrical distribution system in the Mt. Sidney, Ft. Defiance, and New Hope areas. He employed Ralph Gordon to work in the mill and Ralph's son, George Gordon, to help run the electric business. He acquired the remaining half interest for $8,000 on March 12, 1925, when the mill was called the Knightly Light and Power Company, Ltd. The mill produced electricity while continuing to grind flour. It is believed that the residents of Mt. Sidney and Ft. Defiance were provided electrical service within a

Humbert-Knightly Mill, circa 1900

few years. Parts of the New Hope area were not provided electrical service until 1927 because not enough residents would subscribe a sufficient amount of money to help build the line.

The period 1910 to 1940 was a time of rural electrification efforts in America and consolidation in the electric power industry. On December 5, 1931, Minor Garber sold all the property, real, personal, mixed, franchises, contracts, rights of way, easements, privileges, buildings, machinery and equipment to the Virginia Public Service Company. About 1940, Virginia Power discontinued flour milling operations and power generating and razed the buildings, but it retained the land and water and dam rights. Virginia Public Service bought the mill for its distribution system and used it mainly for reserve power until World War II. In the early 1940s, the mill buildings were razed, but Virginia Public Service retained the land, water, and dam rights. Virginia Public Service subsequently became Virginia Electric Power and then Virginia Power of Dominion Resources.

SOURCES: The material for this section was partly based on the book *My Augusta* by C. E. May, 1987, and on an interview conducted with Catherine Garber Crist, daughter of Minor Garber, at her house in Harrisonburg, Virginia, on January 15, 2004.

Humbert-Knightly Mill log dam, circa 1920

Knightly Light & Power Co. Subscription Memorandum

This memorandum is an agreement by and between Knightly Light & Power Co. Ltd., parties of the first part, and all whose names are found below, parties of the second part.

WITNESSETH

The parties of the first part hereby agree to install an Electric Lighting plant for the purpose of furnishing lights to the town of New Hope, also houses on the one line from said plant to destination.

Providing the parties of the second part will subscribe sufficient amount of money to help build the line, which names and money will be placed below of this sheet, and said money to be taken out in lights, money sufficient to do this will average about $40.00 a member.

The parties of the first part will own and keep said line in repair, while the parties of the second part will wire their houses and keep same in good repair.

The parties of the first part agree to put meters in all houses, and there will be a charge of 10 cents per month meter rent or the parties of the second part can buy them and not pay any rent.

Humbert-Knightly Mill, 1927

Knightly Light and Power Company; note electrical transformers in foreground.

The parties of the first part further agree to furnish lights at all times at night, (only when accidents beyond their control should occur, such as high water, etc.) at the rate of 10 cents per Kilowatt as the meter indicates, but the minimum charge will be 90 cents for each month.

Signatures	**Amount**
John D. Western	$30.00
D. T. C. Miller	$40.00
W. F. Fretwell	$60.00
Guy R. Fisher	$25.00
Crawford & Willberger	$40.00
S. H. Bauserman	$25.00
G. C. Beard	$60.00
E. L. Borden	$40.00
T. G. Stout	$40.00
S. C. Miller	$40.00
H. F. Eakle	$25.00
D. C. Cline	$40.00
Chas. W. Garber	$12.00

SOURCE: This blue-stenciled memorandum with original signatures was in the possession of Catherine Garber Crist and she provided it to Wayne Garber who copied it on February 21, 2004.

Ft. Defiance Mill

The Ft. Defiance Mill was established in 1870 on Middle River and was located where Route 616 (Dam Town Road) crosses Middle River and was one of the older, better known mills in this section of Virginia. Previous names for this mill included: Beard's, Wheatland, Cline's, Ellicott, and Old Humbert Mill. A major change in the mill occurred in 1900, when it was converted from a burr to a roller-type machine. The mill was run entirely by waterpower with two large wheels operating horizontally under water. The grain bins had a capacity of 7,000 bushels. All local wheat was utilized in the New Hope milling operation.

The mill's products were famous throughout a wide territory as far south as South Carolina. Mill products included "None Better" and "Cream of the Harvest," both excellent, high-grade plain flours and "Nor-so-na" or "Defiance" brands, both excellent self-rising flours. The mill also did custom grinding for county farmers. W. I. Grove purchased the mill in 1925. By 1947, he was also the proprietor and operator of the Stuarts Draft Mill, Mt. Crawford Mill, and The Plains Mill at New Market, Virginia. The total capacity of the four mills was 310 barrels daily, all high grade products. In

Feed sack from the Ft. Defiance Mill

addition, they produced meal and feed. Four trucks were operated, selling the products of these mills in Virginia, North Carolina, and South Carolina, both direct to the retailer and to the jobber in these states. The mills also shipped a large quantity of their products by rail from the Ft. Defiance Depot.

Until about 1917, the Ft. Defiance Mill was known as the "Old Humbert Mill" and was one of the distinctive landmarks in this section of the state. The Ft. Defiance Mill made a contribution to the New Hope community's economic life by providing stable employment and large purchases of wheat and other grains from area farmers. Furthermore, the company brought in large amounts of outside money through its distribution of products over a wide area. The mill also generated electricity for a short time. The Ft. Defiance Mill was owned and operated by Jim Grove when it was destroyed by fire in August 1960.

Ft. Defiance Mill, originally built about 1870, photo circa 1935

A Flooded Ft. Defiance Mill, 1950s

Ft. Defiance Mill Truck, 1935 with (L-R) Rob Mowry (miller), John Garber (miller), Hugh Hall (truck driver), and Fritz Stout.

Early Houses

During the 1820s and 1830s, the village slowly grew with the building of more houses on New Hope Road near the Stout General Merchandise Store and the Dickerson Tavern.

***Kerr House, eighteenth century**—This house ranks among the oldest standing homes in the upper Valley. The original part of this house was constructed of v-notched logs and followed a two-room plan with one heated room, a single-end chimney, and a hall/parlor with entry into a larger room. Now sheathed in clapboard, the building has a large central stone chimney.*

***Rutledge-Mehler House, circa 1784**—This is a three-bay I-house built with Flemish, three-course American glazed bricks. It has a surviving early detached kitchen and gable end chimneys. The one-room brick kitchen is a one-story, rectangular building with a gable entry and roof, constructed of three-course American bond. The kitchen is now attached to the house.*

Beard House, 1790-92, photo taken 1964 (north view) *—The original part of the house is log construction with two exterior brick chimneys. The high columns were built in 1839 and faced toward a road that is no longer there. After the Civil War, the slave quarters were razed and a new ell built on the east side of the house. In 1910, a front on the west side of the house (the right side in the picture) was created by adding another single-story porch. There are fourteen rooms with a stairwell from the first floor to the attic. The attic contains three rooms.*

Dickerson Tavern, circa 1818, photo taken 1955*—The log part of the house has a two-room plan with one heated room, a single-end chimney, and a hall/parlor entry into a larger room. Over the years, the building has been expanded and altered.*

Fretwell-Garber House, circa 1830, photo taken 1970s*—This two-story antebellum brick covered with stucco, four-bay house has two heated rooms by two end chimneys and entry into one room. A two-story addition was added in the 1850–1870s. The house also had a rectangular side entry outbuilding or washhouse with a gable roof and an exterior brick chimney. Water was piped into the building, spilling into a concrete trough.*

Myers-Eutsler House, 1830s*—This two-story small brick house on the southern edge of New Hope is constructed of seven-course American bond brick. It has exterior decoration of double hound's tooth brick cornice. A one-story kitchen of frame construction was added, and a root cellar exists below one room. This house has a detached kitchen with a large stone and brick fireplace still standing.*

Jim Conner House, 1830s*—This two-story, two-bay antebellum brick house is of Flemish bond construction. It has projecting end chimneys, a gable roof, and 2/2 sash brick cornice. A one-story ell has been added.*

Henry C. Anthony House, circa 1830, photo taken 2004*—This antebellum house is constructed of v-notched logs with some weatherboarding. This was the location of New Hope's telephone company from 1902 to 1921.*

McCullogh-Showalter-Early House, 1830s—*This two-story frame house with two-story ell is pre-Civil War. It is located at the intersection of Routes 616 and 608 and was remodeled about 1910 when the house was raised about one foot and placed on a new foundation. The two exterior chimneys were removed when the house was raised. It was the home of Dr. McCullogh, Dr. Showalter, and Homer Early, founder of the New Hope Garage. The wooden picket fences have accented this house for over 150 years.*

Fretwell House, 1830s—*This two-story frame house originally had four rooms.*

Stout-McCauley House, 1840s—*This house was formerly the home of Dr. William Franklin Stout and was probably built by his father, Thornton G. Stout. In the mid-twentieth century, the house was owned and occupied by the Charles M. McCauley family. The house was one of the most handsome houses in New Hope, but termites invaded the structure and the house was bulldozed about 1965.*

Roberts-Obenschain-Grove House, circa 1845—*This house was built by Dr. William Roberts, a New Hope physician. He owned many acres of land behind the house and built the barn on the hillside. The house was also occupied by the sisters of T. George Stout, who ran the New Hope General Merchandise Store during the middle part of the nineteenth century. The house was occupied by Dr. Clarence Obenchain from 1920–28; the W. I. Grove family occupied the house to the mid-twentieth century. It is a two-story wooden I-house with original two-room plan ells. This house also has a rectangular-shaped washhouse with a two-level gable entry, a gable roof, an exterior brick chimney/flue, and is connected by a breezeway to the kitchen of the main house.*

Fisher House, 1850s, photo about 1960—*This two-story antebellum house was home to Dr. Guy Fisher, a New Hope physician. The four-bay house has four rooms heated by two-end stone chimneys with brick tops and front door entry into both rooms. In the 1880s and 1890s, the Yarborough & Fisher Store was located on this site where the doctor's office is situated. The main house is attached to the original one-room log house and is now used as a kitchen.*

R. M. Simpson House, 1860s, photo taken 1950—*R. M. Simpson was a blacksmith, who lived in this house at the north end of New Hope. His shop was located beside the house.*

Wallace-May House, 1860s*—The original two-room, one-story house was of frame construction with board and batten siding. The date of the original house is unknown, but it was built before 1884. The two-story front addition was added in the late 1940s.*

James White House, 1860s, photo taken 2000*—This frame house followed a two-room plan with one heated room, a single-end chimney, and a hall/parlor with entry into a larger room. The house also had a one-room, rectangular-shaped, one-story outbuilding with gable entry and roof. James White, an African American, came from Nelson County in the late 1800s hoping to find work in the New Hope area. He moved his family into this four-room log house. Later, he added a one-story addition that consisted of a kitchen, dining room, pantry, and porch. Until her death in the mid 1990s, the house was occupied by James' daughter, Irene. Shortly thereafter, it was sold and demolished.*

Clarence Hall House, 1860s, Round Hill area*—The Clarence Hall house is one of the oldest houses located in Round Hill, New Hope's black community. During the late 1860s, some house construction began in the Round Hill area. Surviving Round Hill dwellings date to the late nineteenth and early twentieth centuries and are either frame I-houses, smaller two-room-plan houses or later frame bungalows. This house has a stone foundation and is constructed of hand-hewn, v-notched logs of virgin timber. The logs were covered with weatherboarding and the wood shingle roof was replaced with a tin roof. The two-story house has two rooms on the first floor with a center flue brick chimney and two rooms on the second floor. It also had a hand-dug well as a source of water*

Rinehart-Bauserman House, 1870s—*This two-story wooden I-house was located on Route 617 across from the United Methodist Church. The Bausermans operated the blacksmith shop at the corner of Routes 617 and 608. The house and two acres were bought by the United Methodist Church in 1963, used for church school classes until 1969, and the right front room was used as a pastor's study. In the 1970s, the building was sold and removed and the land is being used for overflow church parking.*

Willberger House, 1880s, photo taken circa 1905—*This is a two-story, three-bay, wooden I-house with original two-room plan ells. It has two interior gable end chimneys.*

New Hope Methodist Parsonage, 1905—*Over the past 100 years, the Methodist parsonage has been home to thirty-two preachers from Rev. C. B. Sutton (1904-1908) to Rev. Douglas Gunsalas (2000-present). The cost to build this Victorian-style house was $1,800. The picture was taken about 1908.*

Garber House, rebuilt 1942 (Former Presbyterian Chapel, circa 1890)—*In 1942, Paul and Ruby Garber bought and renovated the vacated New Hope Presbyterian Church. The preliminary renovation plans based on a house in Waynesboro were drawn on a box cover. The church was located on a three-quarter acre lot, and because the structure was a long building, it was cut in half. The house was built with day labor; carpenters were paid fifty cents an hour and laborers thirty-five cents per hour. The basement was dug out by hand, a coal furnace was installed, the tin roof was sold, and asphalt shingles were installed. The wide pine flooring was relaid and refinished, and the new house was built around the four-and-a-half foot bathtub. The tub, pipes, hardware, windows, and doors were bought from Montgomery Ward in Staunton. The gas stove was an apartment model and the refrigerator had a dent in it. The house cost $5,000 to build and was sold for $10,000 in 1951.*

Charles R. Parr House, circa 1912, photo taken 2005—*This house is located on the southwest corner of the intersection of Routes 608 and 616. The post office was located here from 1897-1908. Charlie Parr was the Postmaster, and he operated a telephone switching service prior to 1902. The toll house was also located at this corner.*

***Michael House, 1910**—The Michael House is located a half mile north of New Hope on Route 608. The house was built by Henry Eakle in 1910 for his daughter and son-in-law, Hugh Garber. Hugh was unable to pay for the house, and it was sold to Eddie Wine. Several years later, Benjamin A. Michael bought it from Eddie Wine. Mr. Michael, or "Mike" as he was known, worked for William "Billy" Franklin Fretwell in the "Old Brick Store" and several postmasters from 1908 to 1925. The post office was located in the brick store at that time.*

***An "adult child" riding the lions**—What drew attention to this house were two cast iron lions that sat on either side of the front walk near the road. These lions were placed there by Michael about 1927 and were admired by people passing by as well as children who loved to ride the lions. James H. Roadcap, Jr., sits on the lion's back.*

New Hope Masonic Lodge

The mid-nineteenth century brought a surge of popularity in fraternal groups throughout the country. It was during these years that many such organizations were begun in Augusta County including the New Hope Masonic Lodge, No. 103, which initially met in the Town Hall building. The lodge was chartered on January 16, 1839, had twenty members, and the officers were Joseph B. Bradford-Master; George W. McCullough, Senior Warden; and John C. Welib, Junior Warden. Below are the lodge rosters for 1848 and 1853.

1848 Roster of New Hope Lodge, No. 103

(Meets at New Hope, Augusta County, on the first Saturday of every month.)

Officers

Thomas Western, Master
James Western, Senior Warden
William R. Roberts, Junior Warden
George W. Peters, Treasurer
William Beard, Secretary
James Bunch, Senior Deacon
George W. Eutsler, Junior Deacon
Charles Batis, Steward and Tiler

Past Masters

William Beard
George W. Peters
Thomas Western
William R. Roberts

Master Masons

John C. Webb
James Murray
James P. Beard
James Turk, Sr.
Andrew Bare
William Turk
Jacob Kyser
Zachariah Johnston
Givens Shifflet
Samuel D. Crawford
Stephen M. Holt
James T. S. McCann

1853 Roster of New Hope Lodge, No. 103

(Meets at Piedmont, Augusta County, the first Saturday preceding the Full Moon in each month and on the feasts of St. John the Baptist and St. John the Evangelist.)

Officers
John Steele, Master
William Baird, Senior warden
David Bunch, Junior Warden
James Western, Treasurer
B. F. Lewis, Secretary
H. A. Johnson, Senior Deacon
John Patterson, Junior Deacon
James Bunch, Steward and Tiler

Past Masters
William Beard
James Western

Master Masons
Givens Shifflet
James Murray
Enoch Coffman
Andrew Bare
George W. Eutsler
A. T. S. McCann
James P. Beard
John C. Webb
Charles Bates
Zachariah Johnston
William R. Roberts
Joseph M. Bishop
Samuel D. Crawford
John W. Palmer
John Kennedy
Albert G. Sigler
Richard Austin
L. T. D. Falconer
William W. Lewis
James N. Gentry
John Towberman
Samuel Black

In 1854, when the lodge became inactive, the past masters were J. B. Bradford, James Turk, Zach Johnston, and James P. Beard. The New Hope Lodge, No. 63, was organized as a re-chartered lodge of extinct New Hope Lodge, No. 103, and was chartered on December 13, 1870. Below is the lodge roster for 1871.

1871 Roster of New Hope Lodge, No. 63

(Meets at New Hope Post Office, Augusta County on the Thursday evening before the full moon, unless the moon falls on Thursday, then on that day.)

Officers
Samuel Kennerly, Worshipful Master
James Western, Senior Warden
Edward J. Jones, Junior Warden
William J. Stout, Secretary
Logan J. Maupin, Treasurer
Abraham Fisher, Senior Deacon
William H. Myers, Junior Deacon
James A. Bunch, Steward and Tiler
J. W. Wolfe, Chaplain

Master Masons
James A. Gentry
David Bunch
John H. Kennedy
Alexander Crawford
William H. Rader
P. A. Fisher
E. M. Nuckles
Samuel Crawford

The peak year for membership was 1876, when there were twenty members. In 1877, the District Deputy Grand Master's (DDGM) report says "the Lodge is in languishing condition" and thinks the location may be the cause. In 1879, the Lodge had seventeen members and the DDGM report says "Officers not bright in ritual, meetings not regular and little degree work done." The 1883 report stated that "Lodge at 11 members, the DDGM recommends surrendering charter, no increase in members, sparely populated area or moving to thickly settled neighborhood." The last annual return from the lodge showed nine members in 1885.

SOURCES: Information regarding New Hope Lodge, No. 103 and No. 63 gathered from *Allen E. Roberts Masonic Library and Museum of Virginia, Inc.*, and provided by Marie Barnett, Librarian. Some information also taken from Ann McCleary, Historic Resources in Augusta County, Va., "Eighteenth Century to the Present, Historic Landmarks of Virginia" (now Department of Historic Resources), 1982.

New Hope Town Hall, built in the 1840s, photograph taken in 1925 with Hazel Early Harner (back right) and her Sunday school class. Also in the back row (left) is Serena Gilbert.

Town Hall Site

With Augusta County's county-based government system, towns did not have their own governing units; however, these towns and villages needed space for community meetings and activities. In the nineteenth century, churches, schools, and fraternal meeting halls often housed some of these functions. The New Hope Town Hall was the first example of a building called a "town hall" in Augusta County. It was located about one half block from the intersection of Routes 617 and 608 on the west side of the road.

We know the New Hope Town Hall existed in the 1840s, but the exact date of construction is not known. We believe the Free Masons built the building and used it until about 1885. On August 10, 1899, the building was sold to the Town of New Hope for $160. The two-story frame building had two floors, was thirty-six feet wide and sixty feet long, and had a central side-entry stairway. The second floor was a single room with benches around the walls; it was used for town and school meetings. The Junior Order of United American Mechanics, a secret beneficent organization that had very small dues, met there every Thursday night. The Woodmen of the World also utilized the second floor for their meetings early in the twentieth century. The first floor had a stage at the north end, a store in the center, bleacher type seats at the south end, and was used for school plays, ice cream parties, and oyster suppers at fifty cents per person. Hazel Harner taught Sunday school for many years at the

New Hope Badge No. 2

United Methodist Church and annually took her class to the Town Hall for an ice cream social. Circuses and carnivals were held in the lot behind the hall.

The Town Hall building also housed the District Courtroom and was used as a jail by the Town of New Hope. Beginning in 1890, New Hope was an incorporated town; during the next twenty years, it had a number of sergeants or policeman and several deputies. On December 20, 1892, the town council authorized the purchase of three police badges. Two of those three badges can be accounted for over one hundred years later. Sonny Hinebaugh, the son of Nelson Hinebaugh who operated the Old Brick Store in the early 1960s, found the sergeants badge in a storage area of the store. The badge in this photograph, New Hope Badge No. 2, was found with a metal detector in a nearby field. It is currently in the possession of Owen Harner.

In the early 1890s, a wooden sidewalk or boardwalk was built on the west side of Main Street (Route 608), beginning at the Simpson house on the north end of the village and extending southward to just past the Town Hall. The street was lighted by kerosene lamps on poles. The wooden sidewalk was gone by the mid-1920s and replaced with gravel. The Town Hall was closed in the 1920s and the building was torn down about 1949. Lawrence and Anna Lee Hildebrand built a new house on the property about 1955.

SOURCES: The information in this section was based an interview with Harry Bauserman in 1977; Ann McCleary, Historic Resources in Augusta County, Va., "Eighteenth Century to the Present, Historic Landmarks of Virginia" (now Department of Historic Resources), 1982, and minutes of the New Hope Town Council, April 5, 1890, to December 12, 1911.

Battle of Piedmont

5 June 1864

Description of the Battle

General Location: Near the village of Piedmont at the crossing of Routes 608 and 778, Piedmont is four miles east of the Valley Pike and seven miles southwest of Port Republic.

Campaign: Lynchburg Campaign (Hunter)

Principal Commanders: [C] Brig. General William E. "Grumble" Jones; [U] Maj. General David Hunter

Forces Engaged: [C] Two infantry brigades (Jones and Browne), home guards, and cavalry under Imboden and Vaughn, about 5,500; [U] Sullivan's division (two brigades under Moor and Thoburn), Stahel's cavalry division, and artillery under DuPont, about 8,500

Casualties: [C] about 1,500 (100 killed/500 wounded/900 missing, etc.); [U] 875 (150 killed/650 wounded/75 missing)

Significance: On 5 June 1864, the U.S. Army of General David Hunter crushed the smaller Confederate army at Piedmont, killing the C.S.A. commander (General "Grumble" Jones) and taking nearly 1,000 prisoners. Piedmont was an unmitigated disaster for the C.S. Army in the Valley. The disorganized Confederates could do nothing to delay Hunter's advance to Staunton, where he was reinforced by Brig. General George Crook's Army of West Virginia marching from the west. United, the U.S. forces moved on Lynchburg. Hearing of Jones' defeat, General Robert E. Lee first rushed J. C. Breckinridge's division back to Rockfish Gap (7 June) and then detached the Second Corps of the Army of Northern Virginia under Lt. General Jubal Early to confront Hunter at Lynchburg (12 June). This detachment severely limited Lee's ability to undertake defensive-offensive operations on the Richmond-Petersburg lines and served to open up the Shenandoah Valley as a second front in the 1864 fighting in Virginia.

Phase One Cavalry Action at Mt. Meridian: Shortly after dawn on 5 June 1864, U.S. Cavalry advanced on the Staunton Road and met C.S. cavalry under Brig. General John D. Imboden at Mt. Meridian. The U.S. troops were driven back until reinforced, then they again advanced to Mt. Meridian, supporting their attack with ten field pieces. The Confederates responded with two guns.

Imboden continued to delay the U.S. advance, while gradually retiring. U.S. cavalry incurred about 100 casualties in the morning's action. Fighting occurred around Bonny Doon. In the wake of the cavalry, U.S. infantry marched south from Port Republic.

Phase Two C.S. Deployment at Piedmont: General "Grumble" Jones deployed his army in an "L" anchored on a bend of Middle River facing north and bending south along the ridge line. He placed his two veteran brigades (under Colonel Beuhring Jones and Colonel William H. Browne) on the left and center behind barricades of fence rails. His reserves, which consisted of home guards, were drawn up in the woods just south and west of Piedmont. Vaughn's cavalry brigade was in position along the Cross Road (present day Route 778) east of Piedmont. His line was supported by artillery. Jones made his headquarters in a tent in the yard of the modern McDonald house. (Imboden's cavalry brigade, after the morning's delaying action, withdrew behind Polecat Draft near Round Hill.)

Phase Three U.S. Advance to Piedmont: About 1,000 U.S. cavalry drove the C.S. troops back to the main infantry line at Piedmont and then withdrew out of cannon range to await the arrival of their infantry and artillery. Moor's brigade arrived first and deployed to the right of the road into the river bend. They were fired on by C.S. skirmishers. Thoburn's brigade deployed to the left of the road in the vicinity of the Shaver House. DuPont arrayed his artillery battalion on the heights confronting the C.S. position. Hunter made his headquarters in the Shaver house. One brigade of U.S. cavalry was held in reserve.

Phase Four U.S. Attacks on the Right: DuPont massed twenty-two guns against the angle in the C.S. line, eventually forcing two batteries to retire and take up a position closer to Piedmont village. Shortly after noon, elements of Moor's brigade assaulted the hill to their right front, driving out the C.S. skirmishers. Supported by a regiment of Thoburn's brigade, Moor's entire line advanced, driving back the advanced C.S. line on the northern brow of the ridge. Jones withdrew his infantry to barricades along Walker's Lane, reinforced his left to meet the U.S. charges, and launched a counterattack. Fighting swayed back and forth across the fields. Hunter now reinforced Moor with Wynkoop's cavalry brigade, fighting dismounted, and renewed his attack.

Phase Five U.S. Attack on the Left: While fighting raged on the right, Colonel Thoburn led three regiments through a ravine and woods on the left and attacked across the Givens Run Valley. Mid-afternoon, he charged directly into a gap in the C.S. line that was opened when Jones reinforced his left flank. C.S. reserves were advancing to fill the gap, but Thoburn's regiment reached the crest first and a savage, hand-to-hand melee erupted. About this time, General Jones was killed, and the C.S. defense came unraveled. Inexplicably, the C.S. cavalry (Vaughn) witnessed Thoburn's attack but did not advance.

Phase Six C.S. Rout: Pressed on the front and rear, Confederate soldiers went streaming over the steep bluffs behind to wade and swim the river. All order was lost. A nasty skirmish was fought over possession of the ford to the rear of the Colonel Crawford house. Stahel's U.S. cavalry division advanced on the far left to close in on the village by the Cross Road. They were met by Vaughn's and Imboden's cavalry who at last came into play to act as rear guard. Some C.S. units attempted to stand near the Middle River Church and at New Hope, and U.S. pursuit gradually slackened. The C.S. army lost about 900 captured.
SOURCE: www.cr.nps.gov/hps/abpp/shenandoah/svs3-9.html

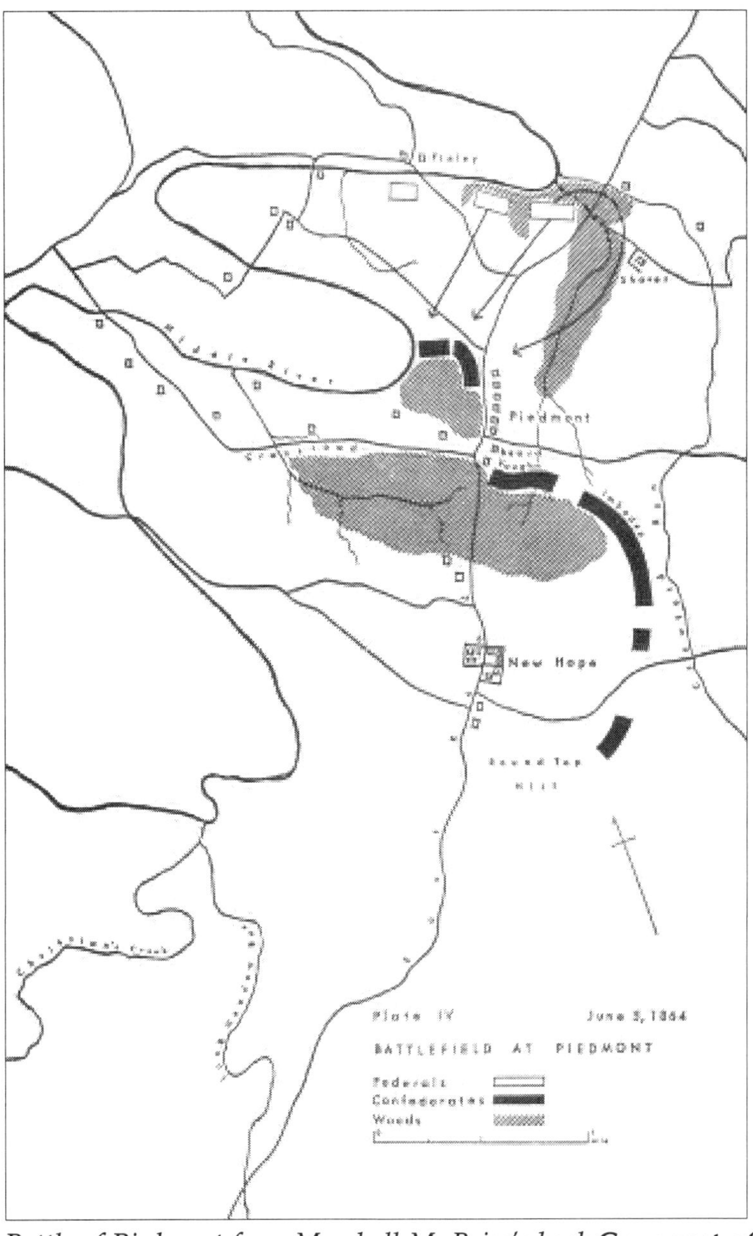

Map of the Battle of Piedmont from Marshall M. Brice's book **Conquest of a Valley.**

History of Cornelius G. Shaver Farm

The farm was bought by Cornelius G. (Shaeffer) Shaver from Isaac C. Myers and his wife Lucinda on February 24, 1847. Cornelius Shaver, a Dunker and pacifist, and his wife, Catherine Hockman Shaver, were from Shenandoah County, near the village of Maurertown. They paid $6,933 for the tract of land situated on the southeast side of Middle River and bounded by the lands of Isaac C. Myers, Crawford, and Mrs. Western. The 267-acre tract was situated northeast of Piedmont and lay on both sides of a spring branch which flows into Middle River. The Shaver family lived in a brick house just east of the site of the present house, which was built in 1856. By the time of the Civil War, the Shavers had numerous children. The oldest were Milton and Mary Emma, teenagers at the time of the Battle of Piedmont.

Cornelius built a two-story, eight-room, ell-shaped frame house facing west on his land with a box tin roof, three chimneys, a central hall, a half basement, front and side porches, and a stone foundation. The four-room ell, attached to the northeast corner of the main block, extends east and has a side porch facing south. The ell contains the kitchen and dining room on the first floor and

Cornelius G. Shaver House, built 1856, photograph taken 1890s*–First Row (L-R) James Shumake, John Shumake, Homer Shumake; second Row (L-R) Mary Emma Shumake, Kittie Shumake, unknown, Sam S. and Frank; third Row (Top) Katherine Shaver.*

two bedrooms on the second floor. The main block contains a living room and parlor downstairs and two bedrooms upstairs. The floors throughout the house are pine boards of varying widths and lengths. The baseboards are eight inches high topped with one-inch molding. The door and window trim and other inside woodwork are fastened with wooden pegs. The fireplaces have simple mantels supported by flat pilasters. The stairway in the main block is decorated with square newels, a railing, and rectangle balusters, and rises from the entrance hall to a landing and then continues to the upstairs hall. A stairway in the kitchen gives access to the upstairs of the ell. Present owners of the house and farm are Mr. and Mrs. Mark Flora. Mrs. Flora is a lineal descendant of Cornelius G. Shaeffer (Shaver), builder of the house.

Battle Account from the Farm

The battle was fought on June 5, 1864, and General David Hunter commanded the Federal forces. After coming under fire, he went with his staff to the Shaver house about mid-morning to seek cover. "When he arrived, Federal skulkers and bummers had been marauding and the women of the household tearfully pleaded for protection. General Hunter decided to establish his headquarters there, ejected the plunderers and put two under arrest." Earlier Colonel Henry A. DuPont had set up several of his guns on the hill above the house. Several of his men entered the house and, seeing two compotes of freshly picked strawberries, took them up to the gun emplacements, ate the berries, and then broke the compotes on the gun barrels. Only one lid survived.

The family took cover in the kitchen, which was located in the basement. The house had little damage, but cannonballs left their marks on the tin roof, bullets lodged in the weatherboarding and one outside door, and a cannonball hit one chimney. Twelve chickens were killed by an exploding shell in the chicken yard.

General Hunter directed the battle from the front porch and the roof over the porch which was easy to get to from the window on the second floor. After the defeat of the Southern forces, General Hunter and his staff departed to go to the village of Piedmont where they spent the night. Wounded soldiers were brought to the house and the granary, probably several dozen. Colonel William Browne and Major Richard Henry Brewer were treated by Thomas A. Reed, a surgeon with the 31st Pennsylvania Infantry, and Henry Knole of the 60th Virginia Cavalry C.S.A. Both men died of their wounds. Hunter's victory in this battle gave the North possession of the Shenandoah Valley and Lee's granary and led to his surrender at Appomattox the following spring.

On September 28, 1864, General George Armstrong Custer, serving under General Philip Sheridan, burned everything that was of use to the Rebels. They arrived at the farm and set fire to the barn and drove away all the livestock.

Many buildings were burned that day; a dozen plumes of smoke and flame were visible on the nearby farms and villages where [flour] mills were located. As a result, times were hard for the Shaver family in the years following the war. They sold land they had elsewhere to pay the taxes levied during the Reconstruction. **SOURCE:** Battle account written by Nellie Shumake Flora (a Shaver Family descendant) and partly based on a book entitled *Virginia Yankee in the Civil War.*

Letter Written after the Battle of Piedmont

It was on Sunday, June 5, 1864. We went to bed Saturday evening as usual. Some time in the night the cavalry gathered around the house. When I got up Sunday morning the yard fence was hitched full of horses and the soldiers were lying on the porch and in the yard. Mother said there would be a battle here today and the soldiers said the Yankees were coming up the road and they were going to try to stop them.

So Dan Scrogham and myself got the horses and ate breakfast and by that time we could see them coming back of Crawford's orchard. We took the horses to the woods. By this time the Minnie balls commenced flying pretty lively. The clover was in head about knee high. The Southern men formed a line across the field after being driven back from the road, but this time from east to west about 400 yards south of the house, while the cavalry was east toward the timber. I was rather between the two armies; they were about 500 or 800 yards apart.

The Southern men then went back up on the hill and formed a line in Walker's land, now where Dan Cline's new house stands. They took the fence on one side of the road and piled it on the other side and made a kind of breast-work; the line ran from the big road west across the hill to the river. This was General Jones' division. General Imboden went back the road about a mile and formed a line east with his division. Jones and Imboden holding the same office, they didn't agree as to position.

About 10 o'clock A.M. the Southern men came down the road below Piedmont with six pieces of artillery and fired six shots at the Yankees who were on the hill back of Billy Crawford's orchard. We were a mile off. The first shot the Yankees fired went across the trees where we were. About a mile from the Southern artillery were the Yankees. When General Hunter got on the porch he could see the situation and put his men in a line across the field near where Dan Cline's house now is. The armies were 400 or 500 yards apart. The Yankees had put some cannons about where John Driver's orchard now is to knock the fence and breastworks down. There were by this time six cannons in our orchard and about twenty pieces of artillery in the field near where we were.

But it got too hot for us and we went farther in the woods. Things were getting pretty lively by this time. General Jones was killed about 2 P.M. while

Piedmont Battlefield Marker

writing a dispatch, about 150 yards west of the road, just north of Piedmont. Col. Brown took his place. General Hunter sent several pieces of cannons up the creek to get endwise to the Southern men. General Imboden was too far back to do much good. Pretty soon the Yankee cavalry went up the hollow and got in behind the Confederates, it was then about 3 P.M. A lot of men ran across the river in Frank Walker's bottom to the woods [now R. C. Byers]. One man told me there was corn in the bottom nearly waist high and the bullets cut the corn like hail and one bullet hit his canteen.

The Southern army lost about 800 men and the Yankees considerable more. There were about 1,100 men taken prisoners. The Yankees took them down in our field and built a rail pen around an acre and put them in it and the cavalry camped around it that night. Colonel Brown was shot in the thigh. They brought him to our house that evening. Wednesday evening he died.

I saw Monday morning where about 1,500 guns were burnt on two piles. A little incident happened Sunday evening. Mr. Roberts went out of the cellar to drive a hog out of the cornfield. The Yankees told him to stop, but he ran in the cellar. The Yankees shot at him and burnt him on the side. They took him prisoner, he said like a hog.

Wednesday morning Dan Scrogham and I buried a man up in the woods. After dinner four of us buried a horse in Crawford's stable in the barn and one in the yard near the stile. There were 60 or 70 wounded soldiers in the barn and house and in the shed. There were 60 to 70 up in the church and schoolhouse and some in Piedmont. The wheat was out in heads and the army made roads through it just where it suited.

While there were cannons just east of the house and the Yankees around the house no bullet hit the house, but the fence was hit 34 or 40 yards on either side of the house. The Yankees had three or four regiments that were not in the fight. I think it was badly managed on the part of the Southern generals. The Yankees were about whipped and ready to quit, but when General Jones was killed, they soon found it out and that encouraged them and that was the time they ran cavalry around behind the Confederates.

Signed: M. H. Shaver

SOURCE: Taken from letter in possession of Miss Cora Garber and Mrs. Ada Reid.

What We Did on Wednesday after the Piedmont Battle, June 8, 1864

On Wednesday morning Dan Scrogham and myself went to the woods and buried a man who had been shot on Sunday. About the middle of the day we put Col. Brown in the coffin, when we put him in the bottom of the coffin he was about to burst out. I got the hammer and drove six ten-penny nails in the bottom while the men held it up with the dead man in it.

In the afternoon four of us went to Mr. Crawford's barn to move a dead horse out of the feeding room where some wounded soldiers lay. We tore down the troughs and rack and buried the horse in the stable, and then we buried a horse at the stile. While we were at it, a man came walking from the spring with a bandage around his head. The doctor told him to raise the bandage. The bullet went in his head just above his cheek on one side of his head and came out on the other side (there were some of the muskets loaded with a ball and three buckshot, it was buckshot that went through his head). I asked the doctor why it didn't kill him. He said it might have happened a hundred times and killed the man, but it didn't cut an artery; he would be able to go home in a few days. The doctor wanted us to carry a wounded man to Mr. Johnson's, about a mile. We put the man on a stretcher and started. When we got to the road the Yankee cavalry came along; one of the men asked us why we were not in the army. Jim Phillips told him we belong to General Bushe's command. The soldiers wanted to know where that command was. One of the soldiers says, "Will, ain't you got any sense? He means they are hiding in the mountains." Then the man we were carrying commenced cursing us and abused us all the way down. I told him I thought wounded as he was he had better think about dying. It just made him worse, and he said we ought to be shot. So you see the cruelty of war.

On June 5th in the morning it was a nice lovely day. The clover was out in head; everything out in bloom, and in the evening the country was full of dead and wounded men and a number of dead horses lying over the fields. The wheat and grass were cut and mashed down. I can't forget the suffering soldiers. Some of the prisoners on the way to prison were killed in a train wreck and thrown in a ditch.

Signed: M. H. Shaver

SOURCE: Taken from a letter in the possession of Miss Cora Garber and Mrs. Ada Reid.

Author's Note: Milton Henry Shaver was born August 28, 1847, near New Hope, Virginia, and died September 8, 1928. He grew up in the period of the Civil War, witnessed the Battle of Piedmont, and escaped being in the last few months of the war by crossing the Ohio River. Milton joined the Church of the Brethren when twenty years old, while visiting his grandfather, Elder George

Shaver, in Shenandoah County. He married Barbara Miller, October 26, 1871, and to this union was born four daughters and one son. The son died in infancy. Shortly after Milton was married, he was elected to the deacon's office. He was frequently called on for advice, supported mission work in Albemarle County and canvassed through the Valley for Bridgewater College. Milton lived his entire married life on his farm near Mt. Sidney and did not give up an active life until within a week of his death. He was a Sunday school teacher continually for more than thirty years and was an agent for the Brethren publications for nearly twenty-seven years.

Staunton Spectator Newspaper Clipping

Communicated

Field Infirmary, Augusta Co.

August 21st 1864

To the Ladies of New Hope and its Vicinity

In behalf of the wounded soldiers who were left at this Infirmary, I return you my sincere thanks for your kind attentions and invaluable services. While in a state of extreme destitution, without food and many without clothing and with no means of communication with our authorities, you came to their relief and administered to their wants with an energy and liberality that have at all times characterized our southern women. Most of the recipients of your kindness have been sent to their homes and will there relate to greatful relatives the history of your benevolence and hospitality. Some have been returned to their commands and will often enliven their camp fires with glowing descriptions of their treatment while in old Augusta. Some of them now fill the patriot's grave and in their last moments blessed the hands that soothed them. To all this you have added the sublime sacrifices of Christianity. Like the good [Good] Samaritan of old you have "bound up your enemies' wounds" and "poured in the oil and the wine." In Hospitable acts, charitable deeds and Christian devotion you have no superiors. Long may you live and enjoy the fruit of your labors!

I would notice particularly the names of the following who (that) were indefatigable in their attentions, viz: Mrs. Col. Crawford, Mrs. Thomas Walker, Mrs. Sallie Johnston, Mrs. Sallie Stout, Mrs. Livie Marshall, Misses Martha Walker, Lucy Stout, Cornelia Stout, Martha Rankin and Sallie Crawford.

CHAS H. HARRIS, Asst. Surgeon in Charge

Letter from Civil War Soldier Staying in Fretwell Tavern

New Hope, Va.
July 21, 1864

Dear Wife,

I was wounded on the 5th day of June by a shell in the knee. I suffered greatly with it for two weeks and on Saturday the 19th my leg was amputated above the knee. It did fairly well and I improved both in strength and hopes of getting back home again to my family. On Sunday three weeks after my amputation my leg began to swell. Then the doctors began to poultice it with warm read [red] oak. It run very freely but it did the swelling no good. The swelling is so great and is not going down at all and if there is no change in a few days I cannot bear it but a few days.

My friend W. D. Greenway is with me and will see to my property. I have on hands $230 Two Hundred and Thirty dollars in new issue and $40 forty in old issues. I have been at private house ever since I have been wounded and will maybe have to pay some of it out. I have a note in my pocket book on Lieut. McGuire of Three Hundred $300 dollars, one on John E. Cummyham for ten $10.00 dollars, one on John Green belonging to the Brass Band $70 dollars, [and one] on John Loving $500 Five Hundred dollars. Have a gold ring I wish you to wear and five nice buttons for Ella and other little one.

Will mention I also have a fine mule worth fifteen Hundred dollars that Mr. Greenway will sell for me. He is doing what ever he can for him. [I] have been at Anna Fretwell's for nearly six weeks. [I] Have been kindly treated ever since I came to her house. She has done all in her power for me whom I highly honor as a lady and my high respects shall be bestowed on her as she has been always by my sick bed all day and night. Have a saddle, bridle and halter worth 150.00 to 200 dollars.

I wish you would send this to my mother and tell her and my brothers and sisters for me good-by. Dear wife and child, I have to write you this painful news that perhaps this is the last letter you will ever receive from me on this earth.

Signed: David Wall
Written by: W. D. Greenway

SOURCE: Letter provided by Isabell Willberger.

Letter of Response from David Wall's Wife to Mr. W. D. Greenway

Madisonville, Tenn. January 29th 1866

Dear Friend,

Your kind favor of 12th inst. came to hand but a few days since. I was truly glad to hear from you. It is the only letter I ever received from you. I received the letter which you wrote for Mr. Wall on the day of his death, after the elapse of three long months. It was a long time to be in suspense, not knowing whether my dear husband was dead or alive or into whose hands he had fallen – friends or foes. I can not express the true gratitude I feel towards you and that kind lady for your kindness to him during his long and grievous affliction. How much I regret that I could not be with him but it is a great satisfaction to know that he was well cared for. I have just received Mr. Wall['s] pocket book containing fifteen hundred dollars in Confederate money with a few other articles, a receipt for his coffin, but none for his board. Did you pay for it or not? I am anxious to know about that and all the particulars whether he felt prepared to meet death and what leg he was wounded in.

I have had a hard time, the Yanks camped on my farm and destroyed, of course, all they could get but I have still had enough to live on. I have two little daughters, the youngest about nineteen months old; she is a dear sweet little child, the image of her father.

Brother Jo has just returned home and has been refugeeing ever since the surrender. He was indebted in several cases had to compromise one suit and the others were thrown out of court. This County is more quiet than any other front of E. Tenn. It is crowded with refugees. A Brigade of Yanky [Yankee] cavalry camped on father's farm 15 days, burnt and destroyed his farm very much. His loss during the last two years of the war was considerable but all our losses here were nothing to compare to loss of my kind husband, David. I have another favor to ask of you. I heard that Wm McLier of Knoxville was living in Baltimore and Mr. Wall has a note on him for seventeen dol. [dollars] given in the year 1857 I think, I wish you would see if you could get any money from him or if the debt could be made for I need the money. Sister kept say [saying], she remembers you very well and often thinks of the pleasant days she use to spend with you all.

This leaves the family in usual health. They all wish to be remembered to you. I hope to hear from you soon.

Yours Truly
M. A. Wall

P.S. I had forgotten to ask you if you were married or not, reports say you are but I think if you was you would have said something about your wife. If you ever come to Tennessee you must be sure and come to see me. I think if I could see you I would ask you about a thousand questions. You must excuse this badly written letter for I am writing where there is no fire and the weather is freezing cold.

Your friend
M. A. W

SOURCE: Letter provided by Isabell Willberger.

Letter from David Wall's Wife to Mr. Fretwell

Madisonville June 1st 1866

Mr. Fretwell
Dear Friend,

I received a letter from you dated February 28th which I replied to immediately and wrote a long letter but have not received any answer yet. I thought perhaps you did not receive any letter and I would write again. In your letter you spoke of having some of Mr. Wall's clothes, which I asked you to express to me at Sweetwater, Tenn. in a bundle as it would cost more to have them boxed and money is very scarce with me. I have sent to the depot several times but nothing there for me. I am anxious to know if Mr. Walls felt prepared for death.

I feel I can never express my gratitude due Mrs. Fretwell and yourself for the kindness bestowed upon my dear husband during his sickness. I have often thought how strange it was that Mr. Wall was born and raise[d] in Va. and had been here but a few years and then sent back there to be kil[l]ed. You will please keep his grave marked. I want to have some tombstones put up there if ever I get able. There is some debts I have to meet first. And our stock and everything we had was destroyed that the Yanks could get and what notes we had before the war some of the men are dead and the rest are broke up and I think it doubtful.

If even I get anything and what was made in Confederate times are all void so it leaves me in low condition. As I have an opportunity of sending this to the office this evening I will close this laconic letter with many kind wishes for yourself and family. I remain your friend.

M. A. Wall

SOURCE: Letter provided by Isabell Willberger.

The Community Grows

In the late nineteenth century, New Hope was the largest village in the present Middle River District and in 1882 was the fifth largest community in Augusta County. The village could not boast of any innovative town planning since New Hope was laid out as a string of lots on each side of the road. Historian John Lewis Peyton described New Hope as a "thriving village" with a population of 200 people. By 1884, the village of New Hope could boast of having forty houses, a graded schoolhouse, post office, a saddler shop, a Methodist church with parsonage, a dunker church, three stores, two blacksmith shops, two resident physicians, and the usual workshops. The Hotchkiss Atlas shows the detailed map of New Hope village with a number of stores, shops, and a Masonic Hall. Since 1884, the general lay-out of the village has changed very little.
SOURCE: With minor modification, the material above comes directly from Ann McCleary, Historic Resources in Augusta County, Va., "Eighteenth Century to the Present, Historic Landmarks of Virginia" (now Department of Historic Resources), 1982.

Chataigne's *Augusta County, Virginia Gazetteer and Classified Business Directory for 1888* states that New Hope had the following:

Magistrate	John G. Gochenour
Supervisor	David Beard
Coach and Wagon Builder	David & Scott
Distiller	Beard, D & Son
General Merchants	Fretwell, F. & Son
	Kerr, Z. T.
	Patterson, J. L.
	Yarbrough & Fisher
Mills - Corn and Flour	Cline, J. M.
	Cline & Wampler
	Ellicott, P. F. & Son
	Sites, Wendall
Undertakers	Scott, John

Principal Farmers: Isaac Coffman, David Beard, John C. Barger, Franklin Barger, Gideon Barnhardt, William B. Crawford, Henry Coiner, James Coiner, Jno. H. Crawford, Noah Early, Christian Eakle, H. K. Eakle, John Firebaugh, Sarah A. Finley, David Garber, S. J. Garber, Levi Garber, William B. Garber, John H. Grove, E. C. Grattan, John C. Humbert, Alexander Kerr, T. Koiner, James T. Kerr, Nathan Kerr, John Miller, J. W. Newman, Dr. Stout & Bros., T. G. Stout, John A. Stover, C. B. Steigel, Windle Sites, B. F. Wampler, Peter Wine, George Wine, Samuel Yount, and Daniel Yount.

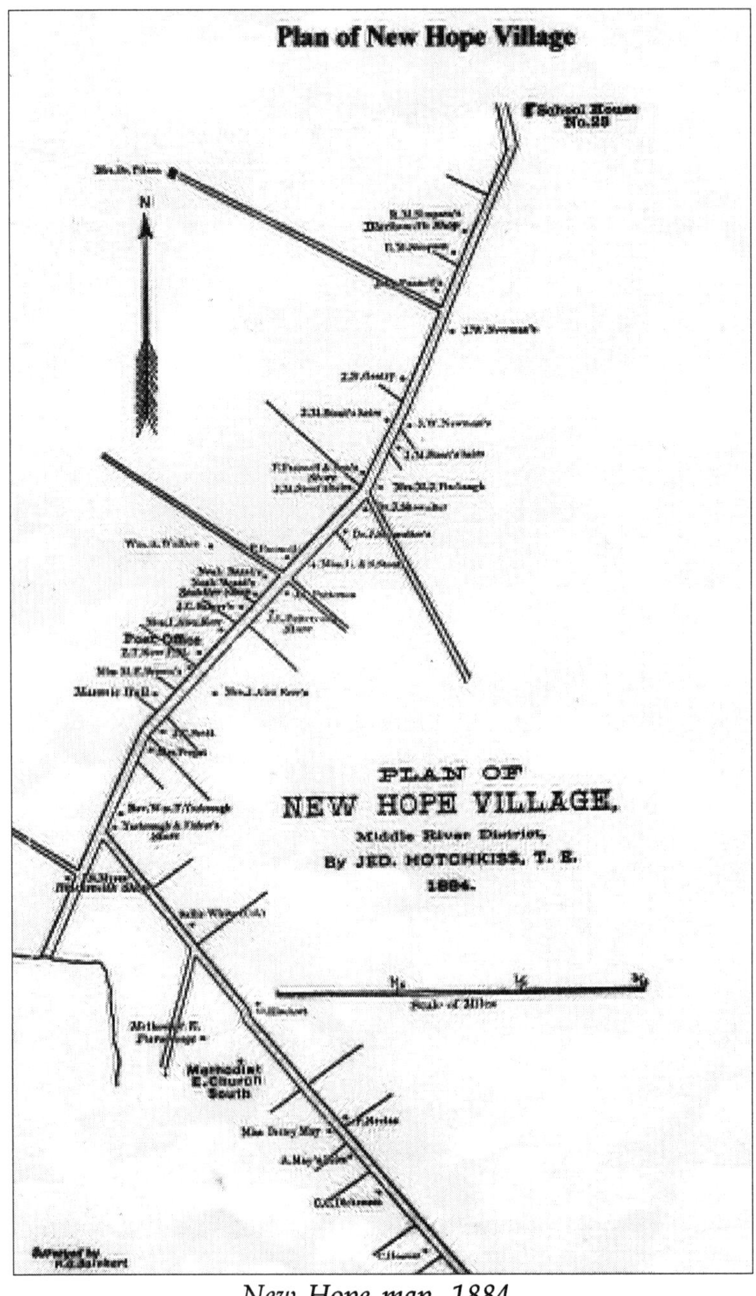

New Hope map, 1884

Education

The history of education in Augusta County spans the antebellum period of private schools and academies to the free public schools built after the Civil War to the eventual consolidation of small country schools into the larger, more diversified schools of the twentieth century. In the nineteenth century, Augusta County took pride in the large number of private academies found primarily in Staunton, which also served some of the needs of the surrounding county. Before the Civil War, New Hope children received their education at the hands of tutors in their homes, through "field schools" organized by groups of families, or at small private schools located in churches or villages. A private school in New Hope stood behind the Fretwell House.

Centennial Public School

After the Civil War the new Virginia Constitution created a mandatory free statewide public school system with the first session beginning in September 1870. With its establishment, a large network of one- and two-room schoolhouses was built across the county for both black and white students. Augusta County had a strong interest in education and established eighty-eight schools by the end of the first year.

New Hope School

New Hope's first public schoolhouse was a two or three-room white frame building that was built in 1870 on or near the present school site. Richard K. MacMaster in his book, *Augusta County History, 1865-1950*, states that the New Hope school had two teachers and two grades (probably primary and intermediate). This school is shown on the Hotchkiss plat of 1884 as School House #23. Unfortunately, no pictures of this school are known to exist, but it was probably similar to the Centennial Public School near Knightly, which was also built in 1870. The Centennial schoolhouse was a two-room school, which had a side entry into a much longer rectangular block and contained a central partition with doors into each room located at the center of the front lateral wall. Two to three windows lined both front and back lateral walls. Other characteristics included interior stove flues and gable roofs. With consolidation of the Augusta County School system in the 1920s, the Centennial Public School became a feeder school to the larger New Hope graded school. Students attended the Centennial Public School through the sixth grade, and the school operated only about five months of the year to allow students to help plant and harvest crops on the farm. The Centennial School closed its doors in the 1930s.

The Second New Hope School, built in 1905, photograph taken in 1908

In 1905, a second New Hope school building was built on the site. The two-story, four-room frame building faced south and was built at a cost of $2,800. It was later enlarged (a home economics wing was added, probably about 1914) with several additions to house an auditorium and grades one through ten; later grade eleven was added. In 1916, a teacher's annual salary averaged $313 per year. One of the upstairs rooms was used for the high school students. We know that a high school class was graduated in 1918, but we do not know if this was the first graduating class. In 1924, the present six-course American bond brick school building was erected as a high school and the frame building became the elementary school. In 1926, the agricultural curriculum was adopted, and the New Hope citizenry built a separate building for this purpose.

By the 1920s, students went to school by various means including walking, horseback, horse and buggy, school wagon, and car. Augusta County provided school transportation for some students by issuing contracts to individuals to drive horse-drawn school wagons.

New Hope High School Graduating Class, 1918: (back row, l-r) Mary Rene Borden, "Gib" Carter, Eldridge Aldheiser; (front row, l-r) Harry Bauserman, Sautelle Ratchford, and Clyde Spitzer.

New Hope High School faculty, 1919-20, names unknown.

About 1920, Daniel S. Garber received a contract to transport school children from the Knightly area to New Hope School. He purchased a truck and built a wooden frame school bus with bench seats that ran the length of the truck bed. He drove the school bus for several years until his death in December 1923.

The second (1905) and third (1924) New Hope schools, photo taken circa 1928

The second (1905) and third (1924) New Hope schools, photo taken late 1930s. The picture shows an early factory-made yellow school bus with bench seats that ran the length of the bus. By the late 1930s, students arrived to school by bus or foot. The horse and buggy days were over. All of the cars pictured here belonged to faculty, not students.

Seen left to right, Berkley Garber, John Quick, Glenna Shaver Powers, an unknown person, Peggy McCauley, and Virginia Andes relax at the New Hope School Chicken House about 1939.

In 1942, an addition was added to the north side of the high school, which included five classrooms, a principal's office, and two bathrooms. About one half of the lower floor was below grade, and the dirt removed for the addition was done with pick and shovel and wheelbarrow. Four men worked several months to complete the excavation. High school students came from Harriston, Crimora, and Waynesboro's northern city limits to attend.

Cartoon depicting the excavation for the five-room addition by Harold Snyder.

In June 1946, an early-morning blaze razed the frame grammar school building and A. C. Gilkeson, Superintendent of Schools, estimated damage at $12,000 to $15,000. Superintendent Gilkeson said the fire is believed to have started in the upstairs room nearest the high school. Principal G. W. Swartz stated that as far as he knew there had been no one in the building for one or two days. He was of the opinion that rats may have caused the fire. He also stated that the cannery, which operated in the basement of the auditorium, would not be in operation until further notice. The frame grammar school building was completely destroyed as evidenced in the photographs on the following pages.

After the June fire, a temporary eight-room school building was constructed in July and August 1946 to replace the frame grammar school. It was a one-story frame building having exterior walls covered with composition material. The wood joist roof was covered with composition material, and the entire building was supported by a brick and cinder block foundation. The interior had a wood joist floor and plasterboard walls and ceilings. The building was lighted by electricity and heated by steam supplied from the low pressure steam boiler located in the brick school. In February 1949, the building was estimated to have an insurable value of $16,000. The temporary school building was razed in 1957 but was not replaced with a permanent building until 1960.

The county began consolidating many of the small country schools by the early 1900s into larger, often brick, schools and high schools in villages and towns. The Augusta County Training School, a consolidated high school, was established in 1938 outside Staunton for African-American students. County schools have continued to grow, both through integration and further consolidation. In 1947, the high school was closed and students were sent to Wilson

Memorial High School in Fishersville. A new brick building was completed in 1960 for primary grades. New Hope Elementary School was closed in 1995, and the building is now leased by the Ruritan Club and the Volunteer Fire Department. On December 6, 1989, Gerald Garber, Supervisor of the Middle River District, spoke to the New Hope Ruritan Club about the future closing of the New Hope Elementary School. He encouraged the Ruritan Club to study the possible acquisition of the school. The club formed an Acquisition Study Committee, conducted a community survey to determine interest in using the school as a community center, and worked with Augusta County to establish a New Hope Volunteer Fire Company and the Community Center at the old school. In May 1996, the Augusta County Board of Supervisors approved a lease agreement between the county and the New Hope Ruritan Club for the

Temporary grammar school built in 1946

grounds of the elementary school. In 1997, the county transferred ownership of the entire school property to include buildings for use as a Volunteer Fire Department and Community Center.

SOURCE: With minor modification, some of the material above comes directly from Ann McCleary, Historic Resources in Augusta County, Va., "Eighteenth Century to the Present, Historic Landmarks of Virginia" (now Department of Historic Resources), 1982.

Teacher Recalls School's Early Days

"Miss Margaret loved birds," Dennis Strole, principal at Weyers Cave Elementary School, fondly remembered about his second grade teacher at New Hope Elementary School. "She kept bird houses and feeders in the window. Every time a bird flew into sight she would stop class and we would watch the bird," he commented. "You could just feel the love," Strole added. Margaret Sites taught at New Hope Elementary School for thirty-eight years, the same school which she attended and from which she graduated in 1922.

"I started to New Hope School in the four-room white building," Miss Margaret recalled of the frame school building built in 1905. "The first floor room to the right of the front door was the primary room – first, second, and third grades. Miss Bessie Kennedy was the teacher. Across the hall was the fourth and fifth grades taught by Miss Sally Stout. Directly above the primary class, Miss Gretchen Bell taught the sixth and seventh grade. The high school students – there was no eighth grade – used the other second floor room. Miss Margaret also remembers that children walked to school or came on horse or in wagons. She and her younger brothers, William and Charles Sites, walked two miles into New Hope. There was a stable on the school grounds for those who came by horse-drawn conveyance. In 1928, a private bus carried children to school for twenty-five cents.

"Each room was heated with a jacketed stove." One of the janitor's jobs was to maintain the fire in each stove. "Each room also had a water cooler. The students would carry water from the well in the village each day. We each had a collapsible cup that we kept at our desk. There was a closet in the back of the school where we hung our coats and kept our lunches," Miss Margaret remembered. "Most of the time we carried hard-cooked eggs or a fried egg sandwich and crackers for lunch." Lunch lasted an hour and students could eat wherever they pleased – inside or out. Children used the time to play familiar games such as softball and Crack the Whip and some unfamiliar games like Prisoner's Base, Tap-the-Rabbit, Fox and Geese, and Ante Over. "When you played Ante Over, six children (would) get on one side of the coal house and six get on the other. One would throw a ball over the coal house. If someone on the other side caught the ball, they could capture a player from the other side." Skirts and "middy" blouses were popular among the girls, making them look like sailors. Boys did not wear overalls to school. Everyone was required to wear shoes. "The girl basketball players wore black sateen bloomers," Miss Margaret noted.

The former teacher recalled some of the school's rules: "no chewing gum, no smoking on school grounds, no fighting on school grounds, and no loafing before or after school at either of New Hope's two stores. The worst thing children did was use tobacco or roll cigarettes in the stable," she added. A story once circulated that some boys got into hard cider they brought from home.

School rarely closed for inclement weather. "In 1918, it snowed in October and didn't melt until April. School closed that year for three months, from December through February," Miss Margaret reminisced. "But not because of the weather. Schools were closed because of the flu epidemic." Another difference Miss Margaret noted was that children did not attend school on Monday. Their week ran Tuesday through Saturday, with Saturday afternoon given to recitation and the literary society.

Margaret Sites graduated from New Hope High School in 1922. "We graduated in the auditorium. Ours was the first graduation exercise ever held at New Hope." After graduation, Miss Sites attended Madison College where she became a member of the Kappa Delta Pi, an educational honor sorority. After two years she had attained a certificate entitling her to teach. Later she returned to college and completed her four-year education. She returned to Augusta County to teach, first at Sampson School, a one-room log building not far from her home. "That first year I earned $60 a month including $10 room and board," Miss Margaret commented. When asked if that was a lot of money in 1924, she answered, "Why no, it wasn't!" She added that her second year she got a slight increase when she moved to a four-room school.

Teachers were expected to comport themselves in an exemplary manner. As Miss Margaret explains, "This was and is a community of churchgoing people. You were expected to conduct yourself in a Christian manner." She returned to her alma mater New Hope her third year, where she taught second grade until her retirement in 1968. "I always used and believed in phonics to teach reading," Miss Margaret commented about her teaching methods. "And

I always let the text book be my guide. I love birds, too, and like to keep bird feeders." "I enjoyed every minute of it," Miss Margaret said firmly. The she corrected herself. "Well, there were some terrible days, but I love children, and I enjoyed teaching."

SOURCE: Sue Simmons, "Teacher Recalls School's Early Days," *Augusta Country*, May 1995 (Vol. 2, Issue 5).

School Activities

New Hope High School offered many activities including a music program, plays, talent contests, poetry, and an active sports program that featured boys' baseball, boys' and girls' basketball, and non-competitive tennis.

New Hope County High School championship baseball team, 1932. The team beat Vesuvius 2-1 in 16 innings. Nelson Burkholder pitched all 16 innings. Pictured here are: (Front Row, L-R) Frank Early, Mike Riddle, Wayne Scrogham, and Nelson Burkholder; (Back Row, L-R) Warren Rankin, Harry Meyerhoeffer, Bill Spitler, ? Crawford, and Charles Wampler.

Round Hill Schools

After the Civil War, a mandatory, free statewide public school system was created in Virginia, with the first school session beginning in September 1870. These post-Civil War schoolhouses followed more standardized designs across the state. Built of frame construction, these new schools generally boasted a gable-end entry with either one or two doors. Two or three windows with six-over-six sash windows pierced the lateral walls. A central brick stove flue provided heating facilities for a wood stove. Decoration proved to be minimal on most of these schoolhouses. Even after the introduction of consolidated schools in the early twentieth century, one-room schoolhouses were gradually abandoned but often continued in use until the 1940s.

School Building A, probably built 1915 – 1925

School Building B, probably built around 1870

During the period of school segregation, the New Hope community had two school buildings at Round Hill for black students. School A was a one-story frame building having a wood joist roof covered with metal. The entire building was supported by a concrete foundation. The interior had a wood joist floor, wood lath, and plaster walls above wood wainscot and wood lath and plaster ceiling. There were no provisions for artificial light, and the building was heated by a stove vented to a brick chimney built from the ground. The estimated value of the building in February 1949 was $1,500. The building contained one classroom.

School B was also a one-story frame building that contained one classroom. The building had a wood joist roof covered with metal and the entire building was supported by a stone foundation. The floor was of wood joist

construction and the sidewalls and ceilings were of wood lath and plaster. There were no provisions for artificial light and the building was heated by stove vented to a brick chimney built from the ground. The building was in a fair state of repair and the estimated insurable value as of February 1949 was approximately $1,500. In 1961, the Round Hill schools were closed.
SOURCE: Augusta County School Board insurance notebook, 1940s.

Blacksmith Shops

There is a mistaken belief that blacksmiths spent all their time shoeing horses. Blacksmiths worked with iron to make or repair the tools that were necessary for farming, including horse and oxen shoes. They also made the tools that were necessary for the daily tasks in the household e.g.; pots for the fireplace, hinges, teakettles, and plow blades. When roads where established in America, the blacksmith repaired wagons and carts. It took a diversity of skills and talents for a village to grow and the blacksmiths represented such. Blacksmiths were very much valued and respected because no village could have continued to exist without them. Many other trades could not exist before the blacksmith opened his business because he repaired the tools of all other people. Blacksmiths in America prospered until the Industrial Age made small enterprises all but obsolete. By the late 1800s, the railroads had linked the country and hardware was manufactured at plants and sold in hardware stores. When the automobile came, the last days of the wagon makers were numbered and had ended by World War I.

Photograph taken around 1900; the man under the shed is Whit Bauserman, son of the owner, Samuel Hilton Bauserman.

Myers-Bauserman Shops

Business at the Bauserman shops started before 1884; photo about 1900.

Samuel Hilton Bauserman operated a wheelwright shop, blacksmith shop, and paint shop at the intersection of Routes 608 and 617, across the street from Dr. Guy Fisher's House. The shop was owned and operated by J. S. Myers in 1884 and probably dates to the early nineteenth century.

Simpson's Blacksmith Shop

R. M. Simpson's blacksmith shop was located at the north end of New Hope and appears on the 1884 Plan of New Hope Village by Jed Hotchkiss. The blacksmith shop was probably built during the middle part of the nineteenth century but the exact date is not known. Ashby "Smut" Simpson, R. M. Simpson's son, operated the business during the 1920s to the 1940s. He also bought and sold hides, which was a very good business in those days. The main hides he dealt in were possum, muskrat, fox, and pole cat. School kids often trapped these animals and brought the hide to Mr. Simpson's shop on the school bus. A quarter for a possum and a dollar for a No. 1 pole cat looked good to a school kid. The fragrance of pole cat was always present in the north end of the village. The shop was torn down about 1955.

The Simpson shops shown in this undated photo were operating before 1884.

East Augusta Mutual Fire Insurance Company

Origin

Though the actual date of the organization of the East Augusta Mutual Insurance Company (E. A. M. I. C.) was June 4, 1870, a group of twelve men had met in New Hope in February 1870 to lay initial plans for such an organization. These were representative citizens from the area surrounding New Hope, in the eastern section of Augusta County. Inasmuch as this was almost exclusively an agricultural region, the signers of this paper were mainly farmers, who were vitally interested in protecting their homes and farm properties and whose vision and concern extended to the interests of the entire community. Realizing from observation of the other insurance companies that individual disasters could be cushioned partially by absorption of any loss by a large body of property holders, they envisioned a mutual organization of farmers who would provide such protection. Thus this small group assumed the initiative in inviting all of the neighbors and fellow citizens of this broad community for the organization of a mutual fire insurance company.

The names of eleven of the twelve founders are known: David Coiner, Jr., James D. Coiner, Michael A. Coiner, Samuel C. Garber, Thomas J. Gilbert, John H. Grove, Samuel Hunter, John D. Miller, Henry Sniteman, Jonas Wampler, John Wine.

Organization

Apparently the hundred names of subscribers had been obtained in short order; on Saturday, June 4, 1870, in the Town Hall, New Hope, Virginia, the organization was affected. A notice was published in the *Staunton Spectator* on May 25, 1870. A general meeting of the subscribers to the E. A. M. I. C. was held at New Hope on Saturday, June 4, 1870. Isaac S. Myers was called to the chair and A. E. Pierce appointed secretary. On motion, a committee of five was appointed to draft a constitution, consisting of A. E. Pierce, Noah Early, Jacob Coffman, Martin Garber, and Enoch Brower. After some deliberation, the committee produced and read a constitution which, after some alteration and amendments, was unanimously adopted. Article 2 stated, "The limits of this company shall be from the Valley turnpike in Augusta County and the Greenville road on the West, and the Albemarle and Nelson line on the East, and from the Rockingham line on the north to the Rockbridge line on the South. Thirty-three days after this organization meeting, insurance of the 100 plus members "commenced at 8:00 o'clock A. M. on the 7th of July, 1870."

Early Meetings 1870-1871

Five weeks after the beginning of insurance coverage, a called meeting of the company was held on August 13, 1870, in the Barren Ridge Schoolhouse.

Matters pertaining to growth, type of insurance, limits of company area, charter, and other items were considered according to the minute book. The secretary read the proceedings of the last meeting and reported the number of members to date as 122.

Amount of valuation $170,136

Amount of insurance to date $113,424

"On motion, resolved that the company apply to the Legislature of Virginia for a Charter of Incorporation and the following members were appointed a committee to carry out the resolution: A. E. Pierce, Daniel Yount, K. B. Koiner, W. T. Yarbrough, and Tobias Weller." "On motion, the company refused to extend the boundary of the company." The following persons in villages applied for insurance: T. G. Stout, J. C. Barger, William H. Myers, and F. Fretwell in New Hope and Wm. Shumate in Mt. Sidney. On motion they were all refused for the present.

According to the minute book, the company held its annual meeting on May 27, 1871, in New Hope. "On motion, resolved that the officers for the present year be a President, Secretary, and nine Directors, who shall constitute the Board of Directors to transact all the business of the Company for one year." The original officers and directors were then elected:

Officers:
Samuel J. Garber, President
E. Pierce, Secretary
Christian Cline, Treasurer
Directors:
Ruben A. Garber
Tobias Willer
A. H. Kindig
John Rubush
Jacob Coffman
Jos. M. Brown
H. G. McCausland
Daniel Shreckhise

The company charter had been received and was accepted by order of the board of directors. The Charter stated that:

- The Capital Stock of the Corporation shall not be less than $75,000.00, in shares of $25.00 each, which may be increased from time to time to a sum not to exceed $200,000.00.
- The principal office of the said Corporation shall be at New Hope, Augusta County, Virginia, and all its business shall be done in said county.

The first insurance policies written by E. A. M. I. C. were issued to its first president. The initial entries in the original policy book carry the following notations, all in the name of Samuel J. Garber:

#1 Wooden dwelling house 28 x 22 ft., 2 stories, with kitchen attached 18 x 18 ft., both in good condition; valued $900, insured $600.

#2 Swisher barn, about 40 yards from dwelling, 78 x 42 ft., stables in basement; in good condition; valued $970; insured $650.

The entire constitution and charter were predicated upon the principle of mutual aid among neighbors. Nothing in the organization records would indicate any desire to make a profit from operations. In actuality, expenses of the company were virtually non-existent for nearly four years. The first fire loss was announced to the board of directors in session at New Hope, May 2, 1874: "The Secretary announced officially the accidental burning of T. J. Maupin's dwelling house on March 14, 1874, which was insured in this Company for $900.00. The levy has been made." The membership of this rural company increased due to the diligence of the directors and by 1875 had reached 355. Losses for the first ten years of operation totaled $6,047.73.

Annual meetings of the stockholders continued to be held in the Town Hall at New Hope until May 4, 1878, when, on recommendation made by the president, the site of the meetings was changed to Staunton. It was stated that "When this company was first organized it was proper that its principal meeting place should be in New Hope, Va., because its birth was in the vicinity of this village and for several years no property was insured at a very great distance from its base. But soon its bounds became extended, until now it is known and has its hold in all parts of the county, so that its principal office is now located at a point inaccessible to a large number of its members, on account of the distance they would have to travel to reach the point at which the meetings are now held."

On July 9, 1894, a parallel company was established to insure the contents of their buildings. It was called the Farmers Mutual Fire Insurance Company. Both companies met obligations until the 1930s when both faced a perilous financial crisis with liabilities exceeding assets. At the annual meeting on May 9, 1931, the stockholders took action by consolidating the two companies, electing a new board of directors, electing new officers, and establishing a central office to conduct business in Room 4, Crowle Building, in Staunton, Virginia. The reorganized company also adopted a policy of classifying risks with rates, advance assessment practices, and the accumulation of permanent safety reserves.

When, on June 4, 1870, the hundred plus farmers assembled in New Hope, Virginia, to organize their company, they were a grassroots organization in the fullest sense and interested in satisfying an imperative need, that of mutual self-protection for their small group. On June 4, 1970, the E.A.M.I.C. celebrated its centennial year. During that century, the East Augusta Mutual Fire Insurance Company grew and prospered and developed because it never lost sight of the fact that it was part of American life. The company has attained its enduring and sustained vitality because it was founded on the basis of the mutuality of humankind. It is still in existence today and the basic principle, that of bearing one another's burdens, has never been supplanted.

SOURCE: *East Augusta Mutual Fire Insurance Co., Organization and Growth, 1870-1970*, compiled by Earl D. Flory

Incorporation of New Hope

The town of New Hope was incorporated effective February 6, 1890, with the passage of Senate Bill No. 144 (see below) by the Virginia General Assembly. The mayor called the first meeting of the seven-member town council on March 8, 1890. The council passed ordinances (see below) and kept minutes of its meetings in a town book. We know from the minutes that the council enforced the town ordinances, levied taxes, assessed many fines for not performing road work and allowing livestock to roam at large in the streets, had a town sergeant (policeman), maintained a police court and jail, hired contractors to help maintain town roads, built a plank walkway (wooden sidewalk) on the west side of Main Street (Route 608), installed and maintained oil street lamps, ordered drainage ditches opened, installed culverts, ordered privies cleaned out, allowed BB cap guns to be fired within town limits, regulated the use of fireworks at Christmas and New Year's, licensed certain businesses, took measures to protect the town people from smallpox in Staunton, imposed fines for disorderly conduct, and bought the Free Mason's interest in the Town Hall. The last entry in the minutes was December 12, 1911. During the town's twenty plus years of self government, the minutes of town council indicate that New Hope had the following mayors; J. H. Shelley, Dr. W. T. Stout, W. T. Fretwell, and H. A. Eakle. The date the town became unincorporated is not known. The authors speculate that it was about 1912 when the town council entered into a contract with Augusta County to macadamize the road through town.

SOURCES: Minutes of New Hope Town Council Meetings, April 5, 1890, to December 12, 1911 provided by B. F. Caricofe, Jr.

SENATE BILL No. 144 (Patron– Mr. Echols)

A BILL

To incorporate the town of New Hope, in Augusta County

Referred to the Committee on County, City, and Town Organizations

1. Be it enacted by the General Assembly of Virginia, That the town of New Hope, in the county of Augusta, shall be and the same is hereby declared

to be a town corporate under the name and style of the town of New Hope, and by that name shall have and exercise the powers hereinafter granted.

2. The government of said town shall be vested in a council of seven, to be chosen annually by ballot on the fourth Thursday in May in each year. Any person entitled to vote in the county of Augusta, and residing in the corporate limits of the town of New Hope, shall be entitled to vote at all elections under said act of incorporation. The mayor shall appoint two members of the council, who, with the clerk of the council, shall hold said election between the hours of sunrise and sunset, and they shall decide any contest with reference to the right of any individual, and shall count the ballots. In case it is impossible to decide the seven who have the highest number of votes by reason of a tie, the said clerk shall decide in the presence of the two councilmen aforesaid by lot. Said clerk shall immediately thereafter make out and deliver to each one of the councilmen elected a certificate of his election.

3. Said councilmen shall meet in the first week of July following, the mayor to be their president. Said officers shall hold their respective offices for one year, or until their successors are elected and qualified. Said officers shall qualify by taking the oath of office before the clerk or other person authorized to administer oaths. They may be removed from office by unanimous vote of the council for good cause. All the officers of the corporation shall serve without compensation, except as hereinafter provided. Said council shall appoint its own time of meeting. Five members shall constitute a quorum, and any vacancy among any of the officers of the corporation shall be filled by said council.

4. In addition to the above-named officers, there shall be elected annually, by the qualified voters of said town, a mayor, a clerk, a town sergeant and treasurer. The mayor shall be the presiding officer of the council, but shall have no vote except in case of a tie, and shall have jurisdiction and authority of a justice of the peace of Augusta county within the corporate limits of said town, and shall be entitled to the same fees. The clerk shall keep a correct record of all the proceedings of the council, shall provide the books and stationery therefor, make out the certificates of election, make out a list of the property to be assessed, real and personal, within the limits of the corporation, and assess the same according to the best information obtained by him; and shall issue tickets for taxes voted by council, which tickets he shall deliver to the sergeant when ordered by the council; and shall have the power to administer the oath of office to any of the town officers, and for said service he shall be allowed annually a certain sum, to be named by the council, not to exceed fifty dollars. The sergeant shall collect the taxes voted by the council, for which he shall be allowed a certain rate per centum for collecting and paying out the same, the rate to be fixed by council. He shall have the power and authority of any con-

stable or collector in the county of Augusta within the corporate limits of the said town, and shall be entitled to the same fees. He shall pay out the money in his hands on the warrant of the mayor and clerk, certifying that it is done by order of the council. He shall perform all the duties of the overseer of roads and streets in the corporation, in accordance with the laws of Virginia. No road tax shall be assessed upon the property within the corporation except by the council aforesaid, which road tax shall be expended upon the roads and streets of said town by the sergeant aforesaid, under the direction of the council; provided said town supports its own poor. For his services as overseer of said roads and streets he shall be entitled to the same compensation allowed by law to overseers of roads. Said council and sergeant shall have all the powers and perform all the duties belonging to overseers of roads under the road law of Augusta county. The sergeant shall, before he enters upon the duties of his office, execute a bond for the faithful performance of his duties, which bond shall be approved by the council and filed with the clerk.

5. The council shall have power to mark accurately the bounds of existing streets; to lay off new streets, alleys, and sidewalks; to regulate and prohibit the running at large of animals; to provide for order and quiet, and the observance of the Sabbath within the corporation; to provide and protect shade trees; to establish fire department, with suitable and necessary conveniences; to regulate in reference to contagious diseases, and to pass ordinances to carry into effect the object of this incorporation, and to punish the violation of the same by fine and imprisonment; provided further, property for public use may be taken in the manner provided for by law, and for that purpose the council of said town shall have the same jurisdiction for the condemning of land for streets for said town as the county courts has for the condemning of land for roads in the county.

6. The council may annually levy a tax for roads and corporation purposes, which on no property shall exceed fifty cents on the hundred dollars' valuation, except that, on the petition of two-thirds of the freeholders within the corporation, the council may levy a corporation tax not to exceed the amount named in said petition.

7. That any person applying to the county court of Augusta for license to sell liquor of any kind, either, as the keeper of a bar-room, wholesale or retail liquor dealer, within the corporate limits of said town of New Hope, Augusta county, or within one mile of the limits of said corporation, shall produce before the court of said county a certificate of the council of said town, signed by a majority of the council, to the effect that the applicant is a suitable person, and that no good reason is known why said license should not be granted. And the court having jurisdiction shall not grant any license to sell liquor within the limits above described until and unless such certificate be given.

8. That for the purpose of maintaining the police regulation of said town, under the authority of this act the jurisdiction of the corporate authorities thereof shall be and the same is hereby made to extend one mile beyond the limits of said town.

9. The following is hereby declared to be the boundary of the town of New Hope: Beginning at Z. T. Kerr's stable, thence north to W. J. Brown's house, thence northeast to Christian Eakle's house, thence east to the north corner of the New Hope school lot, thence with the school lot line to the east corner of same, thence south to Mrs. M. J. Finbaugh's barn, thence south to the east corner of the Round Hill church lot, taking in all of the church property, thence from the south corner of the church property to the beginning at Z. T. Kerr's stable.

10. W. F. Fretwell, Christian Eakle, W. F. Stout, John D. Fisher, W. J. Brown, D. B. Myers, and unknown are hereby declared and appointed councilmen; W. F. Fretwell as clerk, J. D. Fisher as sergeant, Christian Eakle as treasurer, and J. H. Shelly as mayor of said town, and may qualify before any magistrate or notary public in the county, and thereupon they shall constitute, until the first day of July, eighteen hundred and ninety, the council of said town of New Hope, and as such they shall perform all the duties of said council.

11. All previous acts or parts of acts relating to the incorporation of said town are hereby declared null and void.

12. This act shall be in force from its passage.

Ordinances - Town of New Hope, Va.

Section 1. All male persons from 16 to 60 years old shall work the road two days or pay One Dollar fine for failing to do so, to be collected by the Sergeant as any other tax: and all taxable property real and personal to be assessed and a levy of ten cents on each Hundred dollars worth of property for the benefit of said town, and the citizens to be released from paying the same amount to the county in the form of a road tax.

Section 2. Any person who shall commit any breach of peace, such as assault and battery; exhibition of any indecent representation of any subject or thing; lewd, indecent or disorderly conduct; intoxication; abusive, insulting or obscene language, within the limit of the town shall be fined not less than One Dollar or more than Twenty-Five Dollars.

Section 3. If any person shall, without permission from the Mayor in writing, make any loud and unnecessary noises by the human voice, by drums, horns, trumpets or by any other means whereby citizens may be frightened or deprived of rest or sleep; if any person shall discharge or set off in any street or alley any balloon, rocket, torpedo, pop-crackers, fire-works or any combination of gun powder or any other combustible or dangerous material, or without necessity fire or discharge any gun, pistol or other fire-arm of any kind shall be deemed guilty of a misdemeanor and shall pay a fine of not less than One and more than Ten Dollars.

Section 4. Any person willfully disturbing any meeting of persons assembled to witness any performance, exhibition, lecture or any public worship whether licensed or not, shall be deemed guilty of a breach of the peace, and shall be fined not less than One and more than Ten Dollars; if committed in the presence of an officer he shall be arrested without a warrant, and if necessary to give bail for good behaviour for not more than twelve months.

Section 5. Upon the complaint of any citizen or information given by the Sergeant to the Mayor, that a privy, hog-pen or stable is so placed as to be offensive, he may upon summons returned executed against the owner, fine the owner not less than One and more than Twenty Dollars or order such nuisance to be removed. And if any person shall, after notice of such order fail or refuse to obey the same within the time prescribed (not in any case to exceed ten days without a written certificate from the Mayor) he shall be fined not less than Fifty-cents nor more than Five Dollars for each day such nuisance shall thereafter remain, and he may moreover cause such nuisance to be abated at the cost of the owner, and he may issue execution therefore against the goods and chattels of the owner for the use of the Town, to be collected by the Sergeant.

Section 6. Any person who shall cruelly torture any horse mule or any other dumb brute whether his own or that of another, shall be fined not less than One or more than Five Dollars.

Section 7. It shall not be lawful for any persons to congregate upon the streets of this Town in such a manner as in any wise to obstruct the side walks, and the Mayor of the Town has authority to determine what constitutes an obstruction and shall impose a fine such as in his opinion may be right; no horse shall be tied so as to obstruct the walk or make it dangerous to pass.

Section 8. Any person giving minors any kind of intoxicating liquors or causing it to be gotten for them, shall be fined not less than One nor more than Five Dollars.

Section 9. No hog or pig shall be allowed to go at large within the limits of the town. Any person violating this section shall pay a fine of not less than Twenty-five Cents nor more than One Dollar, and if the owner fails to pay said fine the hog or pig shall be sold for the use of the town.

Section 10. No cow, horse or mule shall be allowed to run at large from sun-set to sun-rise, and if the owner allows such to be the case, they shall be fined not less than Twenty-five cents nor more than One Dollar; failure to pay the same forfeits the stock.

Section 11. If any person shall resist any police officer in the discharge of his duty he shall pay a fine of not less than Two nor more than Ten Dollars, and if any person shall fail or refuse to aid or assist a police officer when called upon so to do by such officer when in the discharge of his duty he shall be fined not less than Two nor more than Ten Dollars. Any person failing to pay any fine imposed upon them, shall be confined in the County Jail for a term to be imposed by the Mayor and as in his opinion would be right.

Section 12. Any person riding disorderly or unnecessarily fast or horse racing, shall be fined not less than One nor more than Five Dollars.

Section 13. Any person running a steam engine through the Town without a proper screen, shall be fined not less than One nor more than Five Dollars.

Section 14. In addition to the above Ordinance, we reserve the rights to all the laws prescribed in the Code of Virginia and other incorporated organizations.

By request of the Council,
W. F. FRETWELL, Clerk.

Highlights from the New Hope Town Council Minutes

Nov. 8, 1890 Town council sent W. F. Fretwell and Mr. Stout to Staunton to have three trustees appointed for the Town Hall.

Nov. 8 Committee appointed to see about lumber for plank sidewalk.

Nov. 22 Lumber for plank walk approved. To be sawed 1 1/4 inches, not less than 12 feet and not more than 16 feet long.

Jan. 2, 1891 Council moved that the jail be relocated J. C. Scott's shop. (J. C. Scott was a wagon/coach builder and undertaker.)

Mar. 7, 1892 A motion to get 3 new lamps (street lights) at a cost of $3.75 with fixtures. One at W. F. Fretwell's Store, one at Shelley's corner, and one at Mr. Kerr's (Zack T. Kerr Store and Post Office) was approved. S. H. Bauserman proposed to buy a lamp for the church (Methodist) if the town furnished the oil. Council approved.

Dec. 20 Three police badges bought.

May 23, 1893 Bid for lighting lamps was given to S. H. Bauserman at $2.00 per month. Low bid for building plank walk $29.27 was given to Charlie Parr.

May 21, 1895 Motion by J. D. Fisher to request the citizens to guard the town to protect it from people who have subjected themselves to smallpox or who have been to Staunton. Carried. All such parties to be kept out of town for two weeks thereafter.

June 7 Motion prohibiting anyone from stopping in the town, who have been to Staunton, for at least 14 days.

Sept. 1898 Town sargent (sergeant) to check on condition of Morgan Brown and see if he has diphtheria. If so, he is to be quarantined.

Oct. 12, 1898 Chair asked to dispose of a case pending between Dr. Stout (mayor) and George T. Stout (brother). Dr. Stout was fined three dollars and (required to) tender his resignation (as mayor). George T. Stout was fined two dollars and a half for striking Dr. Stout and five dollars for contempt of court. (The Town Council rescinded their motion requiring Dr. Stout to resign.)

Aug. 10, 1899 On a motion of Dr. Stout the Free Mason's interest in the Town Hall was bought by the town of New Hope for an amount of one hundred sixty dollars.

Feb. 5, 1911 A motion to give the tax due the town to the county for ten years for the purpose of macadamizing the road through town, also to turn the road over to the county for the same (period of) time. (Council approved.)

Doctors

Small detached shops and office buildings once dotted small towns and villages throughout the county. The Hotchkiss Atlas map of New Hope shows several examples of shops including blacksmith, saddler, and doctor office. By the late nineteenth century, doctors often built small, detached office buildings in their yards. Most were one-story, rectangular buildings with a gable-end entry revealing their commercial functions, and many had a front porch like contemporary store buildings. The two remaining doctor offices in New Hope contain two rooms with interior wall stove flues.

SOURCE: With minor modification, the material above comes directly from Ann McCleary, Historic Resources in Augusta County, Va., "Eighteenth Century to the Present, Historic Landmarks of Virginia" (now Department of Historic Resources), 1982.

The residents of New Hope have historically given a high priority to attracting one or more doctors to serve the community's medical needs. Over the years, a number of doctors have lived and practiced medicine in the village during the dates indicated:

Dr. James Allen (c1790-c1837)
Dr. George W. McCullogh (c1837-1844)
Dr. Hanger (1864)
Dr. William R. Roberts (c1845-1870)
Dr. J. E. Eakle (unknown, died c1899)
Dr. J. E. Arbuckle (c1888-1896)
Dr. F. M. Bennett (1888)
Dr. J. M. Warren (1888)
Dr. J. Showalter (c1870-1884–c1900)
Dr. L. N. Harris (1900-1902)
Dr. William Franklin Stout (c1890-1912)
Dr. Thomas C. Miller (1903-1928)
Dr. Guy R. Fisher (c1919 to 1927)
Dr. Clarence P. Obenschain (1920-1928)
Dr. Haynes (1928)
Dr. Theron R. Rolston (1929-1951)
Dr. William T. Davis (1952-1960)
Dr. Theron R. Rolston, Jr. (1961-1965)

Dr. James Allen

Dr. James Allen, son of Captain James Allen, Sr., inherited his father's 264-acre plantation in 1790, lived on the property, and practiced medicine in the Ft. Defiance (New Hope) area for many years. The notebook of surveyor James Wood contains an entry dated November 21, 1740, in Captain James Allen's name for 264 acres on a branch of Middle River called Allen's Run. Captain James Allen, Sr., received a patent for this property June 25, 1747; neighbors were his brother William Allen, Thomas Stevenson, and John Moffett.

Dr. Allen was born in March 1763, married Frances (Fanny) Erwin in 1793, and died at his residence May 1847 in his eighty-fifth year. He was a ruling elder in the Augusta Stone Church for more than forty years. According to the Katherine G. Bushman Papers (1961-1997), Dr. Allen had four sons, all of whom left Augusta County by the time of his death in May 1847 or shortly thereafter.
SOURCE: Walter Dixon, "The James Allen Families of Early Augusta County" *Magazine of Virginia Genealogy* (Volume 42, Number 1).

Dr. G. W. McCullogh

Little is known about Dr. George W. McCullogh, a New Hope physician. He practiced medicine in New Hope in the late 1830s to early 1844 and lived in the McCullogh-Showalter-Early house at the intersection of Routes 616 and 608. His tombstone was found by the authors in a small clump of woods behind his house. He was a Senior Warden in the Masonic Lodge and was honored for his service to the New Hope community. The Masonic Lodge, No. 103 erected a plaque at the New Hope Town Hall, which read as follows:

Dr. G. W. McCullogh
Born July 12, 1810
Died March 11, 1844
Erected October 15, 1853
By New Hope Lodge 103

Dr. Hanger

There was a Dr. Hanger living and practicing medicine in New Hope in 1864. Mennonite Jacob Hildebrand, who lived in the Madrid area, recorded in his journal on January 4, 1864, "Bro. Gabriel ask(ed) me to go to New Hope for Dr. Hanger for his daughter Sarah." This information was taken from *A Mennonite Journal 1862-1865.*

Dr. William Roberts

Dr. William Roberts practiced medicine in New Hope from about 1845 to 1870, and he built the Roberts-Obenschain-Grove House. He owned many acres of land behind the house and built the barn on the hillside. Dr. Roberts was a member and Past Master of the New Hope Masonic Lodge, No. 103 in 1848. He moved away from New Hope in 1870, but we do not know where he went or why he left.

Dr. J. E. Eakle

We know from town council minutes that Dr. Eakle was a town councilman and died in 1899. We do not know the years that he practiced medicine in New Hope.

Dr. J. E. Arbuckle

Dr. Arbuckle was a town councilman and was living in New Hope in 1896. We do not know the years that he practiced medicine.

Dr. F. M. Bennett

Dr. Bennett was practicing medicine in New Hope in 1888 according to Chataigne's *Augusta County, Virginia Gazetteer and Classified Business Directory.*

Dr. J. M. Warren

Dr. Warren was practicing medicine in New Hope in 1888 according to Chataigne's *Augusta County, Virginia Gazetteer and Classified Business Directory.*

Dr. J. Showalter

We know that Dr. J. Showalter was practicing medicine in New Hope in 1884 and that he lived in the Homer Early House. We do not know when he began his New Hope practice but his practice continued until about 1900.

Dr. William Franklin Stout

William Franklin Stout was born in New Hope on April 20, 1865. He graduated from the University of Virginia and received his medical degree from the same school. On July 24, 1889, he married Lucy McGuffin from the Raphine area of northern Rockbridge County. It is believed that he first practiced medicine in Steeles Tavern for a short time after his marriage. An elderly lady from the Spottswood area stated in 1943 that she remembered him as a very handsome man who was considered an excellent young doctor in Steeles Tavern.

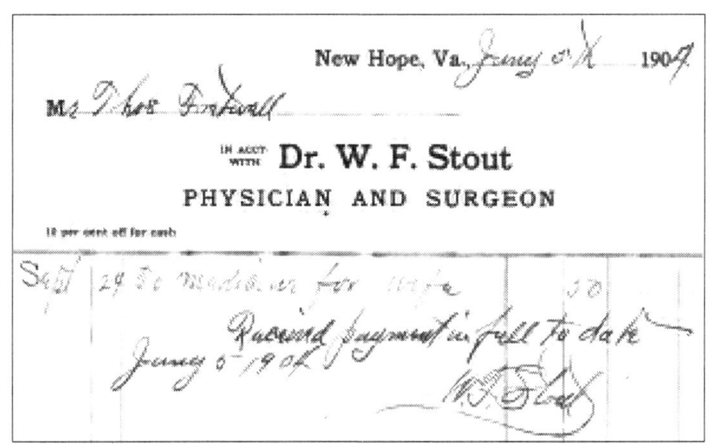

New Hope, Va., 190

M

In Acct with Dr. W. F. Stout

PHYSICIAN AND SURGEON

Received payment in full to date

Dr. Stout's mother stated that William and his family lived in the Charles M. McCauley house in New Hope. She said that William was her doctor and that he was popular. We know that Dr.

Stout was practicing medicine in New Hope in March 1890 because he was elected by the town council to be sergeant and later served as mayor of New Hope. We know from the minutes of the New Hope Telephone Company that "the directors met in Dr. Stout's office in December 1903." The medical office was the one-story white building to the left in the picture. We know that he had stopped practicing medicine in New Hope by the end of 1912. From New Hope, Dr. Stout moved to Charlottesville, married and had a daughter and two sons.

After 1950, Dr. Stout's mother was corresponding with his daughter Elizabeth who said there were no grandchildren and Lucy (Dr. Stout's wife) had died. It is believed that Dr. Stout died in the late 1940s on an island in the Chesapeake Bay (Smith Island) where he practiced medicine.

Stout-McCauley House, built in the 1840s

Dr. Thomas C. Miller

Dr. Thomas C. Miller was born July 19, 1873, to Isaac N. and Mary M. Miller of Goods Mill, Rockingham County, Virginia. He attended Roanoke College two sessions, 1896 and 1897, and then entered the Universal College of Medicine, Richmond, from which he graduated in 1903 and passed the State Board examination. Dr. Miller's long and faithful practice was limited to New Hope and the surrounding community, where he began his practice in 1903. He had a successful medical practice; his skill was recognized and his advice often sought by those of his own profession.

In a deed dated June 12, 1905, Dr. Miller bought seven acres of land in the south end of New Hope from J. W and C. P. Swink and Carol Kerr. He built a house with an office for his medical practice. The office was located in the room on the left side of the front porch.

He did all of his house calls using a horse and buggy, traveling as far as Harriston in all kinds of weather. He had one daughter, Helen, and when she

Dr. Miller's house and office

became old enough to drive, he bought a car. Helen drove him to many of his calls because he was afflicted with arthritis. Dr. Miller practiced medicine in New Hope from 1903 to 1925. He was not able to practice the last three years of his life because of arthritis. Dr. Miller died in New Hope on March 10, 1928, at age fifty-five. He and his wife, who lived from 1877 to 1949, are buried in the St. Paul's Chapel Cemetery at Weyers Cave. The epitaph on his tombstone reads as follows: "His love for humanity was exemplified in his daily life."

He was a communicant member of the St. Paul's Reformed Church, a pledge member of the Phi Chi medical fraternity while in college, a member of the Augusta County Medical Society and a member of Lodge 15 of the Junior Order. His selection as a director in the Bank of New Hope was a tribute to his good judgment and business ability. This was attested also by the fact that he left quite a comfortable estate, property, and insurance.

Dr. Miller's Handwritten Medical Bill to Thuston Borden

Dr. T. C. Miller
New Hope, Va.

1917		
Jan. 19	To one visit	1.50
Feb. 9	To neuralgia tbs.	.15
Feb. 24	To one visit	2.00
Feb. 25	To one visit	2.00
May 14	To Milk Magnesia	.25
July 21	To one visit	2.00
July 26	To milk magnesia	.20
Aug 14	To one visit	2.00
June 5	By cash paid	$10.10

Signed: Dr. T. C. Miller

Dr. Miller, his wife Lillie, and daughter Helen at their home about 1925

Dr. Guy Rothwell Fisher

Guy Rothwell Fisher (b. 1890-d. 1957) was born in New Hope and was a physician in New Hope and Staunton. He was the son of John D. Fisher (d. c. 1925) and Sallie E. Rothwell (b. 1852-d. 1931). He graduated from Covington Grade High School; he then attended Augusta Military Academy, Ft. Defiance, and the Medical College of Virginia, where he received his medical degree. He was a general practitioner in his home community of New Hope for eight years (1919 to 1927); he then specialized for two-and-a-half years at Columbia University Medical School, New York City, receiving an M.S. degree in eye, ear, nose, and throat. He returned to Staunton and enjoyed an exceedingly busy practice. The *Staunton News Leader* reported that Dr. Fisher died on January 16, 1957, and was sixty-seven years old.

Dr. Guy Fisher's New Hope cffice, circa 1885–1910

Dr. Fisher's homeplace and office was located at the intersection of Routes 608 and 617. The property had previously been owned by his father, John Fisher. His father and William T. Yarbrough operated a store on the property. The building above was used as the store and then as Dr. Fisher's office when he was practicing medicine in New Hope around 1915 to 1923. The small building has two rooms with a front porch, is of frame construction, and has a gable roof. The front room was used as an office and the back room as a bedroom. It was reported that the office was moved to its present location and dates to the period 1885-1910.

In Masonry he was a member of three bodies in Staunton: Staunton Lodge,

Dr. Fisher's New Hope office sign

No. 13; AF&AM Union Royal Arch Chapter, No. 2; and Stevenson Commandeny, No. 8 Knights Templar. He joined Acca Shrine Temple, Richmond in 1920, and started in the line of officers in 1941. His elevation to the highest office in the temple, illustrious potentate, took place at the annual meeting in Richmond in January 1945. He attended each succeeding Imperial Shrine Council convention, all of them as an official representative of Acca Temple.

Dr. Fisher was president of the staff of the King's Daughters' Hospital. His other interests in community life included American Red Cross, Staunton-Augusta Chamber of Commerce, Young Men's Christian Association, Augusta County Chapter National Infantile Paralysis Foundation, Augusta County Tuberculosis Association, and Staunton Boys' Club. He was a former president of the Staunton Shrine Club. He was former national president of Circus Saints and Sinners of America, Inc., having previously been president of Hugh B. Sproul Tent in Staunton; he was a director of the former Virginia State Fair, and a member of the Westmoreland Club, Richmond. He also served as president of Staunton Kiwanis Club, as lieutenant governor of Zone 5 Capitol District Kiwanis International; as president of the Staunton Baseball Club, Glenmore Hunt Club, the Men's Club of Central Methodist Church, and once was a member of its Board of Stewards. In 1960, he was state chairman of the Virginia Cancer Society's financial campaign for $235,000.

Dr. Fisher with his sister, Eva (r), and his aunt

Linda Harman sits on a fence about 1946. In the background are Dr. Fisher's New Hope house and office.

In the medical profession many honors had been bestowed upon Dr. Fisher, including: twice president of the Augusta County Medical Association, former president of the Medical Society of the Valley of Virginia, past president of the Medical Society of Virginia, and past president of the Virginia Society of Ophthalmology and Otolaryngology. He was Fellow of the American Academy of Ophthalmology and Otolaryngology, a Diplomat of the Board of Otolaryngology, a member of the American Medical Association, and the Tri-state Medical Society, embracing Virginia and the Carolinas.

Dr, Fisher was a bachelor. His death was ruled a suicide by the medical examiner, Dr. Paxton Powers, who said death was caused by a wound in the temporal region of the head by a .38-caliber revolver. The body was found in his apartment by Miss Mary Mattingly, his office secretary. Dr. Powers reported he could find no explanation for the act, except to speculate that possibly Dr. Fisher had been worrying over his physical condition. He had undergone an operation about a year earlier, but in the intervening time had practiced his professional with regularity, after a period of recuperation. He had recently undergone a checkup at the University of Virginia Hospital.

The Augusta County Historical Society has the Guy R. Fisher Papers, which consist mainly of receipts for items purchased by him from individuals, businesses, and organizations in Augusta County. Of particular interest is a 1932 letter from James Tucker, writing from a jail in Concord, N.C., to Dr. Fisher, asking for his help. Tucker, apparently a former Augusta County citizen, had been jailed for murder.

SOURCE: Based on obituary from the *Staunton News Leader*, 1957.

Dr. Clarence P. Obenschain

Dr. Obenschain was a native of Vinton, educated at Washington and Lee University and the Medical College of Virginia. In 1906, he married Miss Alice Kirkpatrick of the Alone community, began his practice in Rockbridge County, and continued there until 1920. He also served in the Army Medical Corps during World War I. He was a "country" doctor who practiced in New Hope from 1920 until 1928. His medical office was a small stuccoed building with two rooms, a central flue, a gable roof, and a Greek revival mantel in the front room. He owned the Roberts farmstead, which consisted of a bank barn and approximately 100 acres that extended to Round Hill. He lived in what is called

Dr. Obenschain's office

the Roberts-Obenschain-Grove house, and his medical office was located in the house for two years before he built a separate two-room medical office. Before Dr. Obenschain left New Hope, he divided his farm. On September 11, 1928, a land auction was held and the lots between Routes 616 and 617 were sold. He then moved to Staunton, served as the Augusta County coroner for a number of years, chief of staff at King's Daughters' Hospital, and practiced until his retirement in 1945. He died in 1948 at age seventy-two and was survived by his wife and ten children. He was for many years a member of the church council of Christ Lutheran Church.

A Tribute

Never a night too dark, never a road too rough, never a distance too long... that in the words of a close professional friend; rather accurately described the service of Dr. Clarence Phillip Obenschain, who died here recently. Most of his

Dr. Obenschain (dark suit) stands in the middle of his extended family

early practice was in rural areas, Kerr's Creek and New Hope included – night and day, day and night, into the sting of winters sleet and snow, under the surge of summer sun and drenching rain. The urban general practitioner knows something about it, but, in many respects, his education in such matters is not as complete as is that of the "country" doctor. Army Medical Corps captain in World War I, past president of the Augusta County Medical Association, one-time Chief of Staff in King's Daughters' Hospital, years as county coroner; all of these services, but primarily a demanding, heavy practice in country and in city, including perhaps more than his share of charity work, exact a heavy toll. He simply wore himself out, retirement being forced four years ago. Some one called this man a doctor of the "old school." Technically speaking, we would not know; but hundreds knew him for his professional worth that characterized his life and his work.

SOURCES: "A Tribute," *Staunton News Leader*, 1948; obituary of Dr. Clarence P. Obenschain, *Staunton News Leader*, 1948.

Dr. Haynes

We know nothing about Dr. Haynes or his background except that he practiced medicine in 1928 from the little building formerly used by Dr. Obenschain. It is surmised that Dr. Haynes was an interim doctor until the arrival of Dr. Theron Rolston.

Dr. Theron Rice Rolston

Dr. Theron Rolston practiced medicine in New Hope during the 1930s and 1940s. He lived in a comfortable home at Piedmont and his medical office was in the front left room(s) of his home. He was loved by the New Hope community. He died of a cerebral hemorrhage in a Richmond hospital on September 23, 1951.

Dr. Rolston's passing was unexpected and created concern in the community because a rural practice is not appealing to many doctors. His obituary in the *Staunton News Leader* stated "the role of the country doctor is not an easy one. He is unlike the city specialist, with more or less regular hours, regular vacations, and long weekends. For the average rural practitioner it is day and night, followed by a night and day schedule. Dr. Rolston fitted into this demanding routine, and countless occasions found him going to the bedside of patients when he should have been resting or relaxing. A pace like this too often kills, and, at forty-nine, the New Hope physician's practice is concluded."

Dr. Rolston's home and medical office

Dr. Rolston was born in the manse of Hebron Presbyterian Church near Staunton, May 27, 1902, a son of the Rev. Holmes Rolston. He graduated from Washington and Lee University in 1922 and from Medical College of Virginia in 1929. After graduation, he began his medical practice in New Hope from his home office. In 1927, he married Margaret Friend Proctor of Drakes Branch and they had three children. Dr. Rolston was an elder in the Augusta Stone Presbyterian Church, a member of the Augusta County School Board, a member and former president of the Augusta County Medical Association, a member of the Medical Society of Virginia, and a member of the American Medical Association.
SOURCE: Dr. Theron Rice Rolston obituary, *Staunton News Leader*, 1951.

Dr. William T. Davis

A *Staunton News Leader* article on August 12, 1952, stated "New Hope gave its answer to a question that is sorely perplexing hundreds of small American communities when the little town dedicated its new $18,000 Medical Center and handed the keys to the building to Dr. William T. Davis, the young physician whom the modern structure and its facilities have attracted to start his practice. And it was strictly a New Hope answer, because the Center was built with funds raised in the community itself, and there isn't a dollar of state or federal money represented by so much as a single brick." The cost of construction was financed by shares of stock sold to stockholders.

In September 1951, New Hope found itself without a doctor because Dr. T. R. Rolston, who had served the community for many years, died. The Ruritan Club decided that to obtain a doctor in the community there must be some inducement offered. J. J. Hensley, a former Washington contractor, developed blueprint plans for the new medical center. Three trustees were appointed, a trust agreement was developed between trustees and stockholders, $13,685 was raised, and the remainder was borrowed from the bank. The trustees were Howard A Hawkins, Ray Harner, and Tom A. Davis.

The center's upstairs was a spacious, modern three bedroom apartment; on the lower floor was located the doctor's professional quarters, which had a large reception room and four rooms that were used for examinations, laboratory, and the doctor's private office. This picture was taken in 2003.

Dr. Bill Davis was a former resident of Waynesboro and a graduate of Robert E. Lee High School in Staunton. His grandfather, Dr. R. F. Davis, practiced medicine at Hermitage in Augusta County, and his father, Dr. R. F. Davis,

New Hope Medical Center, built in 1952 and closed in 1965

Jr., was a physician in Lexington until his death in 1918. The three generations graduated from the University of Virginia Medical School in 1876, 1910, and 1951. Dr. Davis was finishing his internship in Wilmington, N. C., when he visited New Hope in November 1951 and looked over plans for the new medical center. He had office hours on weekdays from 9-11 in the morning and 7-9 at night with the exception of Wednesday and Sunday. Dr. Davis answered calls as far away as Fishersville, Dooms, Grottoes, Crimora, and Harriston. He began his medical practice in the new medical center in August 1952 and left in 1960.
SOURCE: *Staunton News Leader* article, August 12, 1952.

Dr. Theron R. Rolston, Jr.

Theron R. Rolston, Jr. High school picture circa 1950

Dr. Theron Rice Rolston, Jr. was the son of Dr. Rolston who was New Hope's doctor during the 1930s and 1940s. A letter to the shareholders of the New Hope Medical Center stated the following: "Following the construction of the New Hope Medical Center in 1952 the income from the rent did not provide much more than enough to pay the taxes, interest on borrowed money, upkeep, and small repayments on borrowed money. When Doctor T. R. Rolston, Jr., wanted to buy the property, a meeting of the shareholders was held on April 28, 1961, at which time it was voted to sell the property to Doctor Rolston. When Doctor Rolston decided to give up general practice and accept a position with the Rehabilitation Center at Wilson, he tried to secure another doctor to buy out his practice and property. As he was unsuccessful in this, he sold the property and paid off the trustees in full." In 1965, Dr Theron Rolston left for a clinic in West Virginia. The Medical Center was closed because the community was unable to attract a new doctor and then was sold and converted to a residence.

The above picture was taken about 1950 when Theron was a senior at Woodrow Wilson Memorial High School. In high school his nickname was "Doc," and he participated in Band, Language Club, and Glee Club. With the nickname "Doc" he must have wanted to be a medical doctor at an early age. He had the opportunity to follow in his father's footsteps.
SOURCE: W. Paul Coffman, treasurer for the trustees.

Willberger Funeral Service

In the nineteenth century, funeral homes were generally associated with cabinetmaker's shops, which were located in towns and on farms. Early joiners and cabinetmakers typically made coffins as part of their trade. They often became more involved with the funeral arrangement and entered the business.

The original Willberger Funeral Home reveals a domestic, two-story, two-bay form with cross gable. The main floor was used for services and the second floor to display coffins. The embalming room was located behind the room used for services. An addition was added later on the south side.

Willberger's Funeral Service was founded 1892 by William "Willie" Henry Willberger and operated for nearly 100 years. It was located on Route 608 about one mile south of the center of New Hope and was one of two funeral homes in the northern end of Augusta County. It was later operated by "Willie's" son, Frank (d. 1981), and later Frank's son, James Odie (d. 1969). The last funeral was conducted in 1979.

On September 18, 1982, an auction was held to sell the equipment of the funeral service. The auction included the two horse-drawn hearses dated to the 1880s. There was a wealth of antique funeral industry equipment to include: portable tables used up to the 1940s for embalming bodies at the home of the deceased, old equipment used in the trade, cases of empty embalming fluid bottles, equipment for making boxes used to bury the dead, and lots of coffins and caskets. Toe-pincher coffins are made of wood and are narrow where the head and feet rest, but wide at the shoulders. Caskets are generally rectangular and made of wood or metal. Approximately 150 caskets and coffins were part of the auction.

SOURCE: Based on information provided by Isabell Willberger to Owen Harner

Willberger Funeral Home, established about 1892, photograph circa 1905

Willberger funeral hearse, photo taken 1925

The funeral home owned two horse-drawn hearses, which were used up until the early 1940s. The largest hearse is seen in the bottom photograph while the smallest is seen in the middle photograph.

1956 Series 75 Fleetwood Cadillac Ambulance

1941 Packard Super 8 Hearse

1947 Series 75 Fleetwood Cadillac Hearse

Willberger ambulance

Toe-pincher coffins and wicker body carriers seen at the Willberger auction.

In 1982, Dolly Harner bought one of the wicker body carriers at the Willberger Auction. The body carrier made its way to the California home of Larry Hagman, an actor and star of the TV series *Dallas*. Hagman found a novel and creative use (before and after) for a wonderful antique. Dolly Harner wrote to Larry Hagman and inquired about the fate of the wicker body carrier that she sold. He responded with the letter seen in the photograph.

February 25, 1988

Dolly's Den
Rocky's Antique Mall
Route 11
Weyers Cave, Virginia 24486

Dear Dolly,

Believe it or not, I am writing to thank you.

Enclosed are pictures of my casket and what I did with it. I bolted it to the wall and use it as a bar. What better way to hasten the use of the casket.

At any rate, I just thought you might want to see what beautiful use I made of it, after all, there's really only one other thing you can do with it.

All my very best,

Larry Hagman

Transportation

Roads

Native Americans and wild beasts made the first trails through the Valley as they sought paths of least resistance. Over time, Indian tribes passing through the Valley made a well-marked trail that followed closely the course of the Valley Pike (U.S. Route 11). Indians from New York and Pennsylvania used the Old Indian Trail as they traveled south to trade with the Cherokee and the Tuscarora. As a result of these migrations in and out of the valley, Indian trails developed.

When the settlers arrived, they followed these existing trails and many became the Valley's first roads. The Old Indian Trail running from north to south down the center of the Valley soon became the backbone of the Valley's transportation system as the Great Wagon Road. According to one account, the Old Indian Trail (Valley Pike) connecting the lower Valley to the upper Valley passed through the present Keezletown and Cross Keys. It crossed North River at Beard's ford, crossed Middle River at the Pennsylvania ford, passed through Mt. Meridian, New Hope, Hermitage, Fishersville, and Tinkling Spring and southwest.

A snowy New Hope Road (looking south from Garber's General Store), about 1935

Stagecoaches used the road and traveled from Mt. Meridian to New Hope and then to Fishersville. New Hope's two-lane road, Route 608, was dirt and gravel, and the mud was sometimes too deep for the horse teams. Farmers used the road to drive cattle herds to the mountain to pasture in the summer and returned in the fall. The New Hope Road was not macadamized (paved) until 1912. A toll was charged to pay for the road improvements from New Hope to Ft. Defiance and New Hope to Fishersville. The toll house was located on C. W. Parr's property at the southwest corner of the intersection of Routes 608 and 616W. Bob Dickerson operated the toll house and collected two cents for a horse and rider and five cents for a buggy. Even after New Hope road was paved, the going was sometimes difficult, as evidenced by the snowy scene in the 1930s photograph.

History of Augusta County Road Development

The years after the Revolutionary War brought a flurry of road building accompanying the national interest in improved transportation. Some of the first improvements focused on the Great Wagon Road (Route 11), which was straightened and widened in the 1780s. Although historically it has been called the "Great Wagon Road," historian Robert Mitchell contends that it was not until the 1760s that wagons began to traverse this road extensively; before that time, the road was in too poor condition for regular wagon traffic. Substantial town and village development occurred throughout the Valley, particularly along the wagon road with the road improvements. By 1800, towns in the upper Valley were twenty-two to thirty miles apart and more taverns were established. In 1808, the road through Rockfish Gap became the second turnpike in the state, leading to more improvements in this major east-west artery through the county.

By the early nineteenth century, the state displayed its support for further transportation development by creating the Fund for Internal Improvement and a Board of Public Works to administer the funds in 1816. The board encouraged a more coordinated system of state-wide transportation, including the creation of turnpike charters during the first several decades of the nineteenth century, although not all were completed. In 1824, the Staunton and James River Turnpike Company was chartered to construct a road east to Scottsville, which soon became a market town for local goods. Local farmers sent grain in the form of whiskey to Scottsville to be sent on canal boats to

Richmond. In 1831, the Valley Turnpike Company was chartered to macadamize the road from Staunton to Winchester. The county approved several turnpike charters in 1837. By the 1840s, towns or villages with taverns or other commercial enterprises had developed at regular five- to ten-mile intervals along the Valley Turnpike.

County road improvements kept pace with the expansion of the railroads well into the twentieth century. As residents of one of the state's wealthiest counties, local citizens continually pressed for improved roads throughout the county. The 1885 Hotchkiss Atlas maps show the extensive network of roads that had developed by that date. By the 1920s, Clay Catlett noted that "Augusta County has always had some of the best roads in the state, with more than 350 miles of hard-surface roads, and 12,000 of dirt roads conditioned annually."

SOURCE: With minor modification, the material above comes directly from Ann McCleary, Historic Resources in Augusta County, Va., "Eighteenth Century to the Present, Historic Landmarks of Virginia" (now Department of Historic Resources), 1982.

Railroads

Historically, Staunton has been a transportation crossroads, but the iron horse made a relatively late appearance in the Valley. By 1854, the Virginia Central Railroad (Chesapeake and Ohio Railroad) had been completed to Staunton. The first railroad to come to the Valley (Staunton) was an east-west line, an extension of the Louisa Railroad from Gordonsville. The presence of this railroad made Staunton a key supply depot during the Civil War.

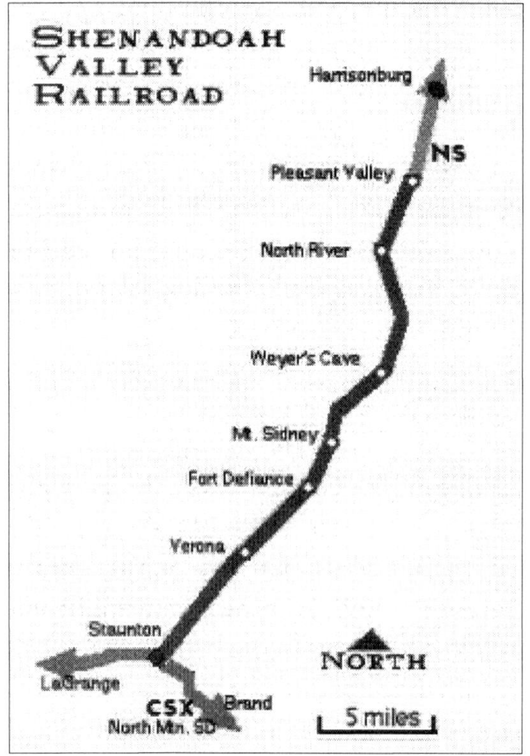

In the 1870s, two major north-south railroads were established through the Valley, both coming from Harper's Ferry. Organized in 1870, the Shenandoah Valley Railroad Company ran through Waynesboro on the eastern side of the Valley. A few years later, the Valley Branch of the Baltimore and Ohio was constructed west of the

Shenandoah River, paralleling the Shenandoah Valley Railroad. This line was once part of the B & O's "Valley Line" that ran from Harper's Ferry to Lexington.

In 1993, the Greater Shenandoah Valley Development Corporation purchased the twenty-mile line from the Norfolk Southern and named it the Shenandoah Valley Railroad. This name was originally used for the railroad that ran on the eastern side of the Valley. Historically, the line began as the Valley Railroad Company of Virginia with Robert E. Lee serving as its first president. The first train traveled from Pleasant Valley, just south of Harrisonburg, to Staunton on March 18, 1874. This short line runs from Staunton to a connection with Norfolk Sourthern at Pleasant Valley. Scenic highlights of the line include stations at Ft. Defiance and Pleasant Valley. The designated line operator is the Buckingham Branch Railroad, which often has two runs per week (Tuesday and Thursday). The line is unsignalled and traffic is limited to ten miles per hour.
SOURCE: www.trainweb.org/varail/shen.html

The emergence of the railroads after the Civil War further boosted Augusta County's economy in the late nineteenth century. Just as the development of the turnpikes led to the creation of many turnpike towns, a number of area villages owe their existence to this railroad. The railroad helped establish new towns such as Basic City (Iron Cross City because the C&O and the N&W crossed there) and Weyers Cave and to further develop older communities like New Hope. The Ft. Defiance Railroad Depot contributed to the prosperity and further development of New Hope by providing farmers with an improved means of shipping their goods to market and area residents with passenger service. According to the *Staunton News Leader*, the Ft. Defiance Depot was touted in mid-March 1910 as the only train station in the world "where the passengers got to ride farther than their tickets call for." The Ft. Defiance Depot could also travel when necessary. The station's wheel-mounted foundation gave it the ability to move backward and forward along its siding, making the loading and unloading of freight much easier.

Various New Hope businesses made use of the Ft. Defiance Depot, which had a passenger waiting room, control room, freight storage space, and an over-hanging slate roof. The depot was of frame construction and featured an octagonal observation projection. The New Hope Garage was a Ford dealer and Model-T cars were shipped from the factory in boxcars to the depot. The partially assembled cars were unloaded, the fenders bolted-on, and the radiator and hood were installed. Gas was put in the tank and the cars were driven to New Hope. The Ft. Defiance Mill shipped barrels of flour from the depot and farmers had boxcar loads of fertilizer delivered to the depot. The Humbert-Knightly Mill had a flour warehouse near the depot for storing flour.

With improvements in the U.S. highway system, the railway industry drastically declined and became mainly a long distance hauler of freight. This led to a huge decline in passenger service and the closing of many freight depots. The Ft. Defiance Depot was closed about 1965; the depot was sold and the railroad right-of-way from Harrisonburg to Staunton was sold to a private concern. Trains still deliver freight to Harrisonburg business as often as twice per week. **SOURCE:** With minor modification, the material above comes directly from Ann McCleary, Historic Resources in Augusta County, Va., "Eighteenth Century to the Present, Historic Landmarks of Virginia" (now Department of Historic Resources), 1982.

Ft. Defiance Railway Depot, 1880s

Steel Truss Bridges

The construction of steel truss bridges represented part of a county-wide program in road improvement at the turn of the twentieth century. Many of the Valley roads and bridges had been damaged and burned during Civil War campaigns. In the late nineteenth and early twentieth centuries, Augusta County pressed for significant improvements in roads and bridges. In 1925, after automobiles had been introduced in the early twentieth century, Augusta County ranked first in the state in the total value of automobiles and trucks, illustrating the local need for good roads.

Kerr's Crossing Bridge (Structure No. 6027), built 1898-1899, photograph 2005

Many steel truss bridges were built in the county between 1890 and 1920. Steel truss bridges served both the road and railroad development at the turn of the century. A 1973 survey revealed that Augusta County had thirty-five steel truss bridges. Until 1932, Augusta County was responsible for the construction and maintenance of its own road system; consequently, it could pick designs and bridge companies. The Kerr's Crossing Bridge is a single-span, pin-connected Pratt pony truss bridge, which carries Route 907 across Christians Creek near the old Kerr house. It was built by the Brackett Bridge Company of Cincinnati, Ohio, and is a significant example of a late nineteenth-century metal pony truss. In 1915, the Champion Bridge Co. of Wilmington, Ohio, built the Knightly Steel Truss Bridge (STB),

Knightly Ford before bridge, circa 1910

a single-span, pin-connected camelback Pratt truss bridge, which carries Route 778 across Middle River just south of Knightly. The bridge is 182 feet long and was one of five STB bridges across Middle River.

SOURCE: With minor modification the material above comes directly from Ann McCleary, Historic Resources in Augusta County, Va., "Eighteenth Century to the Present, Historic Landmarks of Virginia" (now Department of Historic Resources), 1982.

Knightly Bridge (Structure No. 6149) under construction in 1915.

Toll House

Toll houses developed in the late nineteenth century to pay for road improvements (turnpikes), and by the early twentieth century, Augusta County had many toll roads. Early roads were built or macadamized by private contractors and paid for by collecting tolls.

New Hope Toll House

There was a toll house at the corner of Routes 608 and west 616 for collecting tolls from New Hope to Ft. Defiance. The daily cost of a toll coupon was ten cents. The yearly pass for W. H. Willberger to use the toll road until July 1914 for up to two horses was probably about one dollar. The pass was issued on the condition that the holder would slow down when passing through any of the county gates so the gate keepers could recognize the driver or license number of the machine. We have no record of the opening and closing of the New Hope Toll House. It is thought to have operated from about 1912 to 1920.

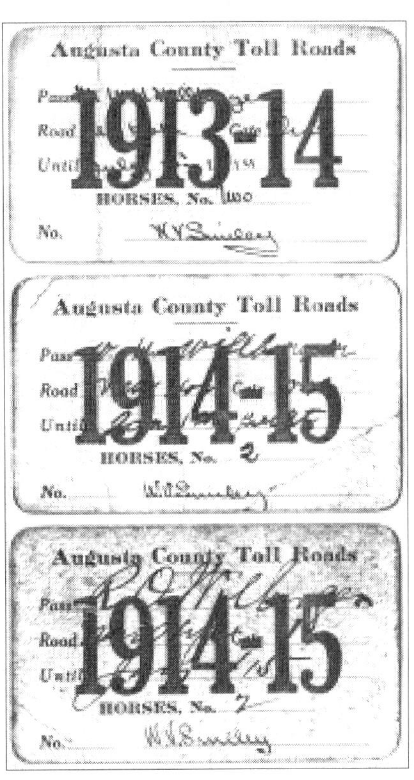

Paul Hunter, left, stands in front of the New Hope toll house about 1918. Right, three years worth of toll coupons for Augusta County roads.

Impact of Automobiles

At the beginning of the twentieth century, the automobile industry was in its infancy. In 1903, Henry Ford was assembling autos one at a time. A few years later, when he introduced mass production, the industry began to boom. The appearance of the automobile spearheaded the drive for improved Augusta County roads for the use of residents and vacationers. Tourists now came to the Valley in great number; in 1928, Catlett noted that Augusta County had a large number of historic and natural tourist attractions. The excellent state of the local highways encouraged more people to come to the area or travel through on their way to the springs. Gas stations and motels cropped up along the major transportation arteries throughout the county. By the 1940s, Routes 11 and 250 were still the most traveled roads by tourists as well as residents. They remained popular until the 1960s, when the construction of Interstates 81 and 64 paralleling the older roads brought traffic from these roads onto the interstates and initiated the building of much larger motels and more fast-food restaurants.

Garages

New Hope Garage

The introduction of the automobile also brought a need for garages. By the late teens, Homer Early realized there was a bright future in the auto industry. Around 1918, he went into business repairing Fords. When WWI ended

Bill Barber (L) and Owen Harner (R) watch as Bob Harner (C) puts water in the radiator of a Model A at the New Hope Garage about 1940.

in 1918, Mr. Early applied for and received an authorized Lincoln, Ford, & Fordson Tractors dealership. The repair shop and dealership was the New Hope Garage. The business grew, and several additions were made to the facility. Model Ts were shipped to Ft. Defiance by rail in box cars. They were not completely assembled when they arrived, so garage employees went to Ft. Defiance to complete assembly by attaching the fenders, radiator, and hood. Gas was put in the tank, and they were driven to New Hope. The business was taken over in the early 1930s by Ray O. Harner. He sold new Fords and used cars and repaired automobiles. The business was operated as a repair shop by Ray's son, Phillip Harner, from 1959 until it closed in 1975.

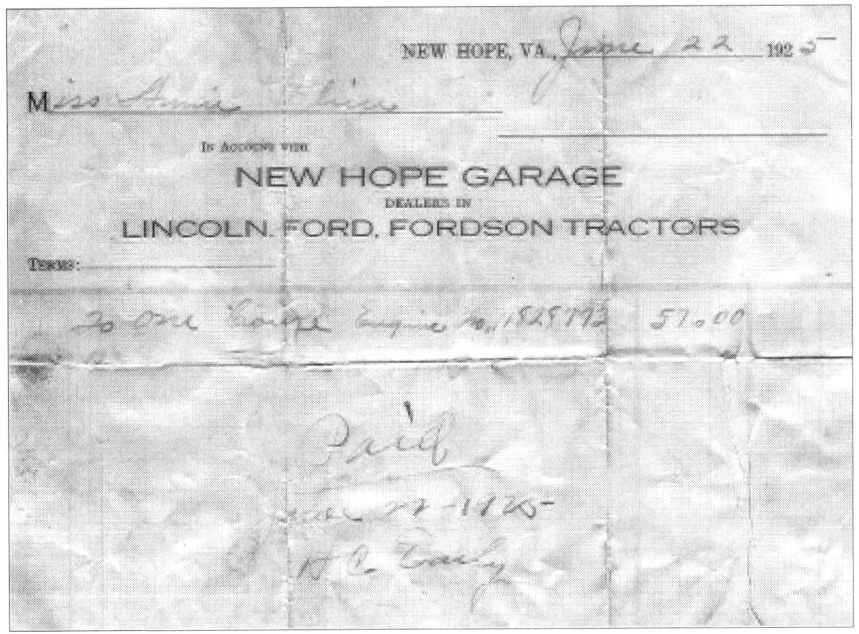

NEW HOPE, VA., June 22 1925

Miss Annie Cline

IN ACCOUNT WITH

NEW HOPE GARAGE

DEALERS IN

LINCOLN, FORD, FORDSON TRACTORS

TERMS:

To One Coupe Engine No. [illegible] 576.00

Paid

June 22-1925

[illegible] Early

The 1925 Ford Model-T doctor's coupe (left) was sold to Miss Annie Cline by Homer Early, owner of the New Hope Garage, for $576, as seen in the June 22, 1925, invoice above.

New Hope Garage, 1920s

Livewire Garage, 1930

In 1930, the Livewire Garage was constructed and opened for business by Claude Spitzer. The garage was located adjacent to the south side of the New Hope School property. Sam Black operated the garage from 1933 to 1938. The garage was closed around 1938. After WWII, the garage housed a cinder block factory operated by John Early and Luther Drumheller for a six- to twelve-month period. It was closed again and not reopened until the 1990s and is now called Early Restorations.

Livewire Garage (today called Early Restorations), photo taken 2005

Gas Stations

The introduction of the automobile brought a need for gas stations and also led to a gradual decay of commercial activities in small towns and villages. In New Hope, the need for gas stations led to the development of several stations including:

- Crossroads (Paxton's) Service Station (1928–present)
- Walter Scrogham's Service Station across from the New Hope School (1938)
- Wine's Service Station beside the Livewire Garage (1925–1947)

These stations used a new building type, which incorporated a small country store. Gasoline was also sold at the New Hope Garage and the New Hope General Merchandise Store.

As more people used automobiles, they recognized the ease with which they could travel to larger towns like Waynesboro and Staunton for their shopping. As a result, country stores, shops, garages, and gas stations began to lose much of their business. Today, most of New Hope's businesses are gone, including two country stores, two garages, two gas stations, and the Bank of New Hope.

History of the Crossroads Station

Jake Coffman's home place was located one mile south of New Hope and had land that fronted the intersection of 608 and 612. With the increase of automobile traffic, he realized that this was a good spot for a gas and auto service station. In 1928, he constructed a building at this intersection and began pumping gas. About 1937, Jake hired Roy Paxton to work for him as a clerk. Around 1940, Roy bought the business from Jake Coffman. In the late 1940s, J. J.

Jake Coffman's Service Station, built 1928, photograph taken 2005

Roy Paxton's Service Station & Store in 2005

Hensley built a new, larger building directly across the road from the original Jake Coffman station. Roy Paxton decided to move his business to the new building location because it offered two gas pumps and space for a larger stock of groceries. The original station was a two-bay, one-story frame building with large glass display windows and a projection carport for gas pumps. With an increase in traffic, the business flourished, and it became necessary to hire a full-time employee. For a few years, he had a mechanic and did auto repair work in the old (original) station, which he had vacated. Roy Paxton spent more than forty years working long hours seven days a week in his gas station business. He rarely missed a day and probably never had a vacation in all those years. Since Roy retired about 1980, his Paxton Service Station has had four different owners, but the business is still going strong. This is one station that has stood the test of time.

History of Eddie Wine Service Station

After a very brief time, Eddie Wine had to give up the ministry because of poor eyesight. He had served as pastor of New Hope Methodist Church for six months in 1922. Then he moved to Collierstown, Virginia, where he served that charge from 1923 to 1924. Eddie moved back to New Hope and in 1925 had a service station built next to the Livewire Garage. It was a typical station for that era with a canopy protruding from the front of the building to cover the gas pumps with space enough to drive between the building and the pumps. There was a grease rack, which was a steel structure two to three feet high over a trench four feet deep that cars could be driven on and serviced from the underside. The station sold gas, oil, fan belts, the usual stocked parts, soft drinks, candy, chewing gum,

Eddie Wine Service Station, built 1925, photo 2005

and other snacks. Several people operated the station to include C. M. "Bus" Drumheller, Oscar Meyerhoeffer, and Ike Bryan (shoe repair and barber shop) until the station and business was closed in 1947. In 1949, the building was bought and rebuilt by Homer F. Garber and Owen Harner as a residence, which it is today. Owen and Dolly Harner lived in the renovated residence until 1959.

History of Walter Scrogham Service Station

Walter Scrogham worked for a number of years as a clerk for Everet Garber in the New Hope General Merchandise Store. In 1938, Garber put the brick store on the market. About this time Walter decided he would start his own business. He bought from Paul Hunter a small lot across from the New Hope School and Wine's Service Station. He had constructed a new service station/store building on the property. Effective July 1, 1939, he was appointed postmaster for New Hope and the post office was located in the service station/store until February 1, 1940. In those days the position of postmaster was a political appointment and this may be the reason for his short tenure as postmaster. He continued to operate the service station until 1943 when the business was closed. Sometime later, the building was bought by Noah Reed and made into the residential dwelling it is today.

Walter Scrogham Service Station and post office, built 1939, photo taken 2005

By 1941 when this photograph of Harold "Jan" Garber, II was taken at the Stout-Fretwell-Garber General Merchandise Store, the automobile had made a significant impact on the life of the New Hope Community. So much so that even this general store sold gasoline.

Twentieth-Century Development

Crawford and Willberger Store

New Hope evolved to support the area's farm economy and became part of the Valley's system of town-centered settlements in the nineteenth century. In 1906, Robert Odie Willberger and his partner, C. D. Crawford, started the Crawford and Willberger Store, a general store located in the center of New Hope. The store was built by Eutsler Brothers for Crawford and Willberger. The building is a two-story, three-bay, rectangular, frame building with shed roof, recessed entry, and stick style false front. It retains the original shelves and counters. A frame side addition was added in the early 1920s.

After his partner died, Mr. Willberger carried on the business by maintaining a large store, which sold almost everything the folks in the area needed. According to one account, a spot check showed the following items for sale: dry goods, chicken and cow feed, motor oil, pitch forks, plow shares, soft drinks, hardware needs, hosiery, groceries, work shoes, dress shoes, a complete line of sewing equipment, and a big line of both work and dress clothes for men and women. The shoe shop (left side) was added to the store in the early 1920s. It was a friendly place and a true genuine representation of an "old country store." During the last half of the twentieth century, Frank Willberger operated the store. After more than seventy-five years of operation, the business was closed and now the building is rented by a cabinetmaker.

Not all retail distribution was issued from towns. Peddlers carried various manufactured items, especially tin-ware and clocks. They traveled through the countryside by horse and wagon during the nineteenth and early twentieth centuries offering their wares for sale to farmers, and they competed intensely with town merchants. These peddlers filled an important niche in the farm economy by saving the farmer a trip to the nearest town. Northern manufacturers used towns like Winchester as warehouse and distribution centers, where peddlers could replenish their inventories. According to local stories, the last known peddler with horse and wagon visited New Hope in the late 1940s.

Crawford and Willberger Store, built in 1906 (top). Notice the automobile and Firestone sign in the bottom 1907 photograph.

Crawford and Willberger Store, west side about 1907

Crawford and Willberger Store, 1906

The shoe shop (left side) was added to the store in the early 1920s and can be seen in this 1995 photo.

New Hope Telephones

Alexander Graham Bell invented the telephone on March 10, 1876, in Boston, Massachusetts, when he made the first telephone call "Mr. Watson, come here, I want you!" The first permanent outdoor telephone wire, strung in 1877, covered a distance of three miles, and commercial telephone service began in the United States. The workable exchange, developed in 1878, enabled calls to be switched among any number of subscribers rather than requiring direct lines. Exchanges were handled manually, first by boys, then by women operators. In 1879, telephone subscribers began to be designed by numbers rather than names. The dial phone was invented in the 1880s by Almond Brown Stroger.

History of New Hope Switchboard Association (New Hope Telephone Company)

The new technology spread fast, and Charles R. Parr had a phone exchange in New Hope by the late 1890s or early 1900s until the New Hope Switchboard Association bought him out and began providing service that continues to this day. On September 6, 1902, gentlemen from the New Hope area met in the District Court Room at the New Hope Town Hall for the purpose of arranging for switchboard service for New Hope. The operator and owner of the existing switchboard, Charles R. Parr, had given notice that he would no longer give exchange (provide phone service). The group also met for the purpose of forming a permanent organization to own and control the switchboard of New Hope so that all

The H. C. Anthony house was the location of the switchboard from 1902 to 1921.

New Hope switchboard office, seen here about 1955.

Guy Borden talking on the phone, circa 1957

might have better service and to promote mutual exchange with other switchboards of Augusta County.

The meeting was called to order by W. F. Stout. C. W. Simms was elected temporary chairman, after which Simms was elected permanent chairman and W. F. Stout secretary. After varied discussions relative to telephone service, W. F. Fretwell set fourth a plan and proposition to build a commercial telephone line from New Hope to Staunton. He moved "That all persons who had payed (paid) two dollars for construction of the [Weyers] Cave and New Hope commercial line, now in operation, be assessed three dollars to be applied to construction of the said Staunton and New Hope commercial line and all other persons having connection with the New Hope Switchboard be assessed five dollars for said construction and that a committee be appointed by this body to sell five or six phone rites (rights) on the Cave and New Hope commercial line at not less than ten dollars per rite (rights), the proceeds of said sales to be applied to the construction of the Staunton and New Hope commercial line. After slight discussion, the above motion was carried. It was then moved that a committee be appointed to ascertain the most practical route." The motion carried and "W. F. Fretwell, G. C. Beard and H. G. Barnhart were nominated and elected as Route Committee." "H. G. Barnhart then moved that parties owning two telephones or more should be assessed for his home phone $5.00 and for each other on separate farms or tracts of land $2.50 but in case said party or parties sold their sight (site) rite (right) to any phone except the home phone, the party purchasing said rite shall pay to the Association $2.50." The motion was carried. The Route Committee was also "empowered to contract with any proper person for the operation of the said Board for one year" and asked to report at the next meeting on September 20, 1902. There was a committee appointed which included H. G. Barnhart, C. W. Simms, and W. F. Stout to submit a constitution and bylaws for adoption by the Association.

A new switchboard operator is being trained by Beulah Wampler (standing) as Tom Davis, a phone company director, looks on.

Edna Baber, relief operator, 1959 talking on the party line.

At the September 20, 1902, meeting, the following officers were elected: President, C. W. Simms; Vice President, W. F. Fretwell; and Secretary, W. F. Stout. After discussion of several proposals for a commercial line connecting Staunton, the Rev. D. C. Flory moved to accept the Port Republic and Staunton road route, which was estimated to cost about $203.50. The motion carried. The committee reported that Miss Nellie Simpson had agreed to give switchboard service for a few weeks at $1.50 per week. It was decided to proceed to build the line to Staunton and also make proper arrangements for establishment of a switchboard at New Hope.

At the October 25, 1902, meeting the Board of Directors was formed and included the officers plus Jno. Wright, Sr.; Rev. A. B. Early; Jno. G. Gochenour; N. L. Shreckhise, and Jno. L. Sites. The constitution and bylaws were adopted. Article I discussed association name, objectives, members, and officers. Article II defined the duties of officers, and Article III discussed called meetings, alterations of the constitution, and election of officers. The bylaws had twelve sections, which are stated below:

Section 1 – There shall be a printed notice furnished by the Association, upon or near every phone, to read as follows: "All persons who do not own a telephone (in service) or do not pay switchboard fees, shall be required to PAY

10 cents for each business message, and 5 cents for each social message; one-half of such fee is to be turned over to the Association. Calls for ministers of the Gospel, Physicians, Funeral Directors, and death messages are to be exempt from the above charges.

Section 2 – The Association shall meet the fourth Saturday in October of each year, at New Hope, Va., for the purpose of electing officers and to transact such other business as may be brought before it.

Section 3 – Term of office shall begin December the 1st of each year and terminate December 1st of the following year provided the offices have been filled by legal election.

Section 4 – Each Telephone Company whose lines directly enter the Association switchboard, shall own, maintain, and control its own line and telephones and collect its own tolls and assessments, but shall pass no rules or bylaws that may conflict with the Constitution and Bylaws of this Association.

Section 5 – Each line connecting with the Association's Switchboard and having no direct connection with any other pay switchboard, shall be required to pay into the Treasury of the Association five dollars for each phone upon such line, provided that the members of such line have not already paid two dollars on the [Weyers] Cave and New Hope commercial line, and in such case they shall be required to pay ($3.00) three dollars.

Section 6 – Any member owning two or more phones on separate farms or tracts of land, (whether the phones be on the same or different lines), shall pay for one ($5.00) five dollars, and for each other one two dollars and fifty cents.

Section 7 – Whenever there has been sufficient money collected under the preceding sections to defray expenses of the construction of a New Hope and Staunton commercial line, the residue shall be applied to the general expenses of the Association.

Section 8 – All lines having no other switchboard connection, with pay switchboards, shall pay to the Association ($3.00) three dollars per annum, payable semi-annually for each phone, on the 1st day of December and June of each year, which shall be for all switchboard fees for New Hope and Staunton.

Section 9 – All lines having connection with two or more pay switchboards shall pay into the Association one dollar per annum, payable semi-annually on the 1st of December and June of each year for switchboard fees at New Hope.

Section 10 – All lines severing connection with all other switchboards (receiving pay) shall at once come under Art. 1, Section 8

Section 11 – The President of the Association shall, with the consent of the Board of Directors, cause any line entering the switchboard to be cut out that does not within thirty days after due notice pay into the Association its dues and assessments.

Section 12 – To defray the expenses of the Association, the Board of Directors may and are empowered to make levies or assessments against each line in the Association, and the Secretary shall notify the President of each line of the amount assessed against each line, but said assessment shall be so made that the same amount shall be levied against each phone on the line.

Excerpts from the minutes of the association from 1903 to 1919.

- The board of directors met on April 20, 1903, in the District Court Room and the following was decided: the Buttermilk line be cut out of the New Hope Switchboard, an appointed committee would confer with Burketown Switchboard regarding mutual exchange, and Jno. L. Sites would be empowered to repair and untangle the commercial lines at anytime. It was also decided that line No. 2 be notified of all dues and assessments and, if the said line does not pay up within 30 days after such notice, it shall be cut out of the switchboard.
- The board met on May 2, 1903, and ordered the secretary to notify all lines of their indebtedness for construction of the Staunton commercial line.
- At the August 4, 1903 meeting the board of directors "ordered the secretary to notify all lines that they would be deprived of service after 9:00 o'clock P. M., August 15th, 1903, if their fees and assessments were not payed (paid) over to the Treasurer by that time."
- The association met in annual session in the District Court Room on October 23, 1903. The president read his annual report, which was of great interest calling attention to the construction of our commercial line to Staunton which was paid for in our first year, an increase in membership and the Switchboard Association only owing $1.53 at the end of the first fiscal year.

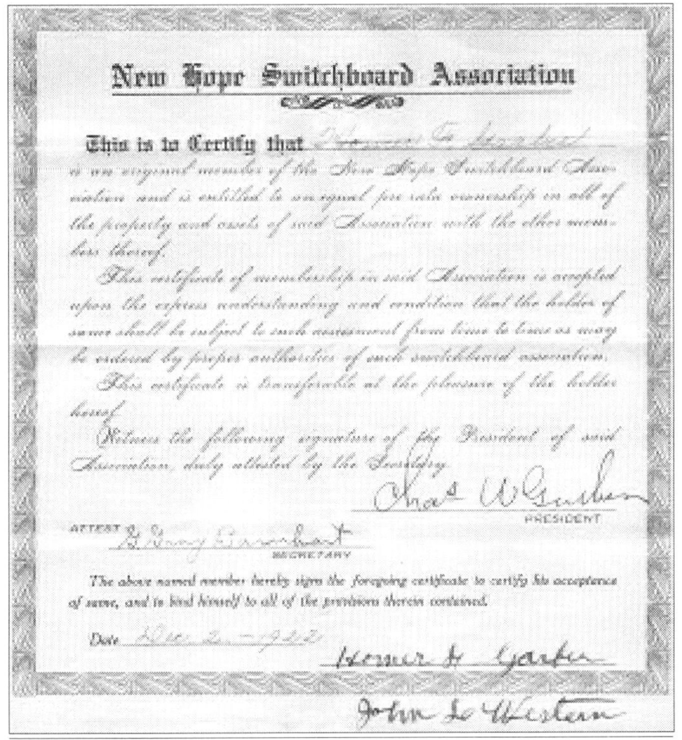

New Hope Switchboard Association

This is to Certify that

is an original member of the New Hope Switchboard Association and is entitled to an equal pro rata ownership in all of the property and assets of said Association with the other members thereof.

This certificate of membership in said Association is accepted upon the express understanding and condition that the holder of same shall be subject to such assessment from time to time as may be ordered by proper authorities of such switchboard association.

This certificate is transferable at the pleasure of the holder hereof.

Witness the following signature of the President of said Association, duly attested by the Secretary.

PRESIDENT

ATTEST

SECRETARY

The above named member hereby signs the foregoing certificate to certify his acceptance of same, and to bind himself to all of the provisions therein contained.

Date

Homer F. Garber's 1922 stock certificate

- The Board of Directors met on December 18, 1903, in Dr. Stout's office. President W. T. Fretwell notified the Board that the appointed committee had contracted for one year with H. C. Anthony for switchboard service at a rate of ten dollars per month and moved the switchboard into Anthony's house, which was across the street from the present location of the telephone company. The board approved the establishment of a pay station in New Hope so anyone could send messages from the New Hope Switchboard. It was agreed that the pay station be located at W. F. Fretwell's store, the cost per message would be ten cents and that the money collected go to H. C. Anthony, the switchboard operator.

• At the January 11, 1904, meeting, the board decided to ascertain the cost of a commercial line to Waynesboro via Crimora and other routes.

• On November 5, 1904, the Association met in annual session in the District Court Room of the Town Hall and decided to make some improvements at the switchboard office for the comfort of the operators. It was also decided that the switchboard would be open by 6 a.m. and closed at 10 p.m. from October 1 to April 1 and from April 1 to October 1 opened at 5 a.m. and closed at 9 p.m.

• The December 3, 1904, board meeting was attended by M. L. Shaver, Daniel Garber, Wm. B. Garber, and John D. Western from line No. 6. Mr. Shaver requested that line No. 6 be divided and have one portion enter Burketown Switchboard and the other portion enter the New Hope Switchboard and each holder be allowed to place a two-pronged switch on his phone to connect to each line. The Board decided to allow the requested change and charge two dollars per year for local and commercial service so long as they (subscribers) pay their service at Burketown. The Board accepted and approved a five-year contract with the Staunton Switchboard for fifty dollars per year to provide line services for up to sixty phones. The Board also allowed phone holders on the Weyers Cave line (No. 5) local and commercial service for one dollar per year provided said line (No. 5) kept the poles in repair for our commercial line between New Hope and Weyers Cave.

• On February 15, 1919, the annual meeting of the Association was held in the Town Hall. This was the seventeenth annual meeting but was not held in November or December of 1918 on account of the "flue" epidemic. "The meeting was well attended and various complaints of service at the switchboard were discussed and plans for better service proposed. Mr. W. T. Fretwell suggested that we investigate plans, etc., to get one man to run the (switch) board and attend all business for us and we (are) looking to him for service." It was moved that the board of directors confer with Mr. Switzer regarding the new plan for better service. "The resolutions passed by the Directors on December 9, 1918 were sustained by the Association by a vote of 26 to 0." The treasurer's report was adopted which showed the Association sixty-four cents in debt.

In 1902, when the New Hope Switchboard Association bought the Parr switchboard it began providing telephone services from H. C. Anthony's house, which is across the street from the present telephone company location. H. C. Anthony was the first telephone exchange operator hired by the phone company.

At the regular meeting of the Board of Directors on January 26, 1921, E. A. Aldhizer submitted plans to build a five-room bungalow, a turn-key job for $1,800. Homer Scrogham was appointed to purchase land for the house. J. A. Hunter had land directly across the street from Anthony's house, where the switchboard was located. This was an ideal site because relocating lines and equipment would be relatively easy. It was a huge undertaking to construct and pay for a permanent building for the switchboard operator and living quarters for the family. As all changes do, it caused considerable disagreement and hard feelings among the 150 stockholders.

At the Bank of New Hope meeting on March 29, 1921, Albert Fisher presented a proposal to the directors to operate the switchboard when it was moved to its new location. Fisher's proposal was very simple: "$50.00 a month pay and coal for heating." The directors were not in favor of furnishing Fisher coal but expected the same number of hours of service. The stockholders met at the Town Hall on April 13, 1921, and voted in favor of hiring Fisher. Fisher's wife, Siggie, would be the main operator. Over the years, the switchboard has had the following operators: H. C. Anthony (1902-1921), Siggie Fisher (1921-1941), Esther Whitmer (1941-1947, Sarah Patterson (1947-1953), and Beulah Wampler (1953-1963).

In the early years (1902-1940s), phone subscribers had wall-mounted phones that consisted of a large (one foot by two foot) wooden box with a bell ringer, a mouthpiece, and an earpiece on a four-foot cord. Until the early 1960s, the telephone company had a party line phone system, which allowed for listening in on your neighbor's phone calls. The old switchboard was replaced in 1963 with an automated switching system. Guy Borden was the maintenance man for many years. The New Hope Telephone Company has had many presidents during its long history; however, no one has served as long as Kelly Chapman, who served as president and board member for forty years.Today, the New Hope Switchboard Association is called the New Hope Telephone Company.

The phone company has now operated for over 100 years and is still locally owned and operated. The founders and early subscribers of the New Hope Switchboard Association included the following persons:

H. G. Barnhart
G. C. Beard
A. C. Borden
Harry Borden
J. N. Click
Kemper Coiner
Rev. A. B. Early
J. S. Early
Rev. D. C. Flory
F. H. Fretwell
W. F. Fretwell
J. F. Garber
J. Luther Garber
Jno. G. Gochenour, Jr.
Jos. R. R. Humbert
Jno. S. Kerr
D. C. Landis
Granville Miller
J. S. Miller
C. R. Parr
S. P. Rinehart
Jos. Ritchie
M. L. Shaver
N. L. Shreckhise
Homer Shumake
C. W. Simms
Jno. L. Sites
J. W. Spitler
H. B. Steigle
C. A. Stickley
W. F. Stout
O. W. Willberger
W. H. Willberger
Jno. Wright, Sr.

Note: The above names were compiled from the early minutes of the association and may not be complete.

SOURCE: Based on review of the Constitution and Bylaws of the New Hope Switchboard Association, adopted October 25, 1902, and copies of corporate minutes.

Bank of New Hope

At the beginning of the twentieth century, agriculture was the primary business with many farms surrounding the village of New Hope. The nearest banks were in Staunton and Waynesboro, so interest developed on the part of area farmers and businessmen to establish a local bank. In 1913, the Bank of New Hope was built and opened for business. The bank boasted masonry construction to aid fire prevention and included elaborate decoration. The one-story building displayed pro-style temple form with six-course American bond brick, a gable roof, fanlight and medallion cornice in the portico, and a brick shed addition along one side.

It has been reported that when the bank opened, money was hauled by wagon from Staunton to New Hope. No records were available to the writers regarding the financial condition of the Bank after 1929. The Bank of New Hope prospered for many years until the late twentieth century. Jefferson National Bank of Charlottesville, Virginia, acquired the bank about 1970. Jefferson National continued to operate the bank as a community branch. With the consolidation in the banking industry during the 1980s and 1990s, Jefferson National Bank was acquired by Wachovia Bank about 1995. Shortly after the Wachovia acquisition, the Bank of New Hope was closed and the building auctioned off in May 1998. The back part of the building and roof were severely damaged by fire in 2000.

Bank of New Hope, built in 1913, photograph taken in 1940

History of the Bank of New Hope

The Bank of New Hope was incorporated by the Commonwealth of Virginia on July 1, 1913, and given a certificate of authority to commence business. Fees paid to the Commonwealth of Virginia included a charter fee of ten dollars, tax and seal of one dollar, Clerk's fee of fifty cents, an entering, issuing, and certifying fee of three dollars and fifty cents, and a recording fee of four dollars. According to the Certificate of Incorporation, the purposes for which the corporation was formed were as follows: To carry on a banking business, and, in connection therewith, to discount bills, notes and other evidence of debt; receive and pay out deposits, with or without interest; to receive on special deposit, money or bullion of foreign countries, stocks, bonds or other securities; to buy and sell foreign and domestic exchanges, gold and silver bullion, foreign coins, bonds, stocks, bills of exchange, notes, and other negotiable paper; to lend money on percentage, securities or bonds, pledges of bonds, or other negotiable securities. To take and receive security by mortgage or otherwise upon property, real or personal, and accept as collateral, security for loans, bonds, secured by real estate. To invest money for individuals or corporations, to do any business, and exercise any powers incident to the business of companies doing a banking business.

The Certificate of Incorporation stated that the minimum capital stock of the corporation was ten thousand dollars, and the maximum capital stock was twenty-five thousand dollars, divided into shares of the par value of one hundred dollars each. The names and residences of the officers and directors, who, unless sooner changed by the stockholders, are for the first year to manage the affairs of the corporation, were as follows:

Officers	**Office**	**Residence**
H. G. Baylor	President	Harriston, VA
A. C. Borden	Vice President	Waynesboro, VA
W. F. Fretwell*	Cashier	New Hope, VA
W. F. Fretwell	Secretary	New Hope, VA

Directors	**Residence**
H. G. Baylor	Harriston, VA
A. C. Borden	Waynesboro, VA
W. F. Fretwell	New Hope, VA
A. B. Early	New Hope, VA
J. W. Wright	Grottoes, VA
J. F. Miller	Grottoes, VA
C. A. Alexander	Harriston, VA
Samuel Yount	Waynesboro, VA
Dr. T. C. Miller	New Hope, VA

* The bank's first cashier was W. F. Fretwell, who owned and operated the New Hope General Merchandise Store formerly owned by the Stouts.

The subscribers to and owners of the capital stock of the Bank of New Hope, Inc., signed a subscription agreement which read as follows: "We the undersigned do hereby subscribe to and agree to pay for in cash the number of shares set opposite our names of the par value of One Hundred $100 Dollars per share of the capital stock of a corporation to be hereafter organized for the purpose of conducting a Bank at New Hope, Virginia under some suitable name to be hereafter agreed on. We agree to make payments on the stock as they may be called for by the directors of the corporation."

Names	**Shares**
Dr. T. C. Miller	5 Shares, $500
J. L. Driver	5 Shares, $500
S. L. Miller	5 Shares, $500
Geo. A. Early	5 Shares, $500
J. F. Miller	5 Shares, $500
J. W. Stoner	5 Shares, $500
H. G. Baylor	5 Shares, $500
A. C. Borden	5 Shares, $500
John W. Spitler	5 Shares, $500
J. W. Wright	5 Shares, $500
D. C. Cline	5 Shares, $500
W. F. Fretwell	5 Shares, $500
D. C. Flory	5 Shares, $500
T. M. Borden	5 Shares, $500
S. H. Driver	5 Shares, $500
Cline Bros.	5 Shares, $500
B. A. Michael	5 Shares, $500
J. F. Strough	5 Shares, $500
A. B. Early	5 Shares, $500
E. L. Eakle	5 Shares, $500
C. A. Alexander	5 Shares, $500
Mrs. Mary S. Page	5 Shares, $500
Annie Laurie Page	1 Share, $100
Crawford Patterson	2 Shares, $200
C. W. Rankin	2 Shares, $200
J. T. Driver	2 Shares, $200
Isaac Spitzer	5 Shares, $500
W. F. Patterson	5 Shares, $500
Samuel Yount	5 Shares, $500
Theo. Coiner	5 Shares, $500
P. H. Cline	5 Shares, $500
D. H. McAllister	2 Shares, $200
W. P. McAllister	4 Shares, $400
W. R. Flory	2 Shares, $200
Mrs. Carrie A. Beard	5 Shares, $500
W. H. Scrogham	4 Shares, $400
C. R. Caldwell	5 Shares, $500
J. S. Norford	5 Shares, $500
Michael Kivlighan	5 Shares, $500
R. O. Beard	5 Shares, $500
W. N. McAllister	5 Shares, $500
Alexander Reed	2 Shares, $200
D. Arlie Cline	1 Share, $100
Mary F. Stiegel	1 Share, $100
John H. Nicholas	2 Shares, $200
J. E. Wine	5 Shares, $500
E. L. Borden	2 Shares, $200
Geo. A. Phillips	2 Shares, $200

Bank of New Hope, photograph about 1975

An organization meeting of the subscribers of the stock of the Bank of New Hope was held on May 19, 1913, at the office of C. R. Caldwell, Room #7, Farmers & Merchants Bank Building, Staunton, Virginia All 200 shares of common stock at $100 par value per share were represented to elect bank officers. "On motion, the following resolution was unanimously adopted. RESOLVED, that the said Certificate of Incorporation or Charter be, and the same is hereby accepted, and that the Officers and Directors set out therein be the Officers and Directors of this Corporation for the current year."

A special meeting of the stockholders was conducted on June 13, 1914, at the New Hope Bank building for the purpose of considering the question of reducing the capital stock of the bank from $20,000 to $10,000 par value. On motion, the resolution was unanimously adopted. As a result of this decision, the stockholder surrendered to the bank all of the shares of stock outstanding on July 8, 1914, and the bank issued one share of stock for each two shares of stock heretofore standing on the books.

At stockholders' meetings the cashier was called on to make a statement regarding the financial condition of the bank and the following was reported:

Meeting Date	Profit to Capital	Profit	Profit & Surplus	Dividend Paid	Stock Book Value per Share
January 8, 1916	7.83%				
January 13, 1917	15.14%				$127.64
January 12, 1918 (1)	21%	$2,087.02		10%	$147.25
January 11, 1919	22%	$2,221.59		10%	
January 10, 1920 (2)	33%		$6,982.53	12%	
January 8, 1921			$9,970.13	20%	
January 14, 1922	31.44%	$3,144.33		16%	
January 23, 1923 (3)	30.86%	$3,086.66		16%	
January 12, 1924	22%	$2,206.55		16%	
January 10, 1925 (4)	29.8%	$2,980.44		16%	
January 9, 1926	26.74%	$2,670.69		16%	$249.68
January 8, 1927	30.5%	$3,059.40		20%	
January 14, 1928	34.5%	$3,460.94		20%	$274.88
January 12, 1929	30.5%	$3,048.86		20%	$285.37

(1) - On motion to pay the Directors $1.00 for each meeting they attended was carried.
(2) - The Cashier reported: dividends paid last three years $3,200.00, deposits at present $145,936.88, and loans $151,546.74.
(3) - The Cashier reported surplus $9,000, reserves $3,150.59, dividends paid to date $8,400, and total profit for nine years $20,550.59.
(4) – An appointed committee drew up a resolution of appreciation for the services of Cashier W. F. Fretwell on behalf of the stockholders of the bank, and the resolution was placed in the minutes of the bank. Fretwell died during the year 1926.

SOURCE: This section based on Corporate Minutes of the Bank of New Hope, 1913 to 1928.

Augusta Dairy Drop-off Station

Area farmers brought their cream and milk in cans to the Augusta Dairy Drop-off Station, which opened about 1925 and operated until 1936. Each can was weighed and tested for butter fat content to determine the price that would be paid to the farmer. The cream also had to pass a "smell" test to detect if the cream was sour or if the cows had been put out on grass too early in the spring. If so, the cream would smell of garlic and was unfit for processing. The unfit cream was not wasted but taken back to the farm and fed to the hogs. After the cream passed all of the above tests, it was combined in large containers with cream belonging to others. The cream was transported to Staunton each morning for processing. George Gilbert, who lived beside the New Hope Telephone Company Office, had a Model-T truck and hauled the cream to Staunton. The cream was not iced or placed in cold water on the truck. George would also haul passengers to and from Staunton for a small fee.

The foundation of the drop-off station remains beside the creek on the south side of New Hope, near the Miller farmstead. The facility had a drilled well, a wooden water tank that stood eighteen feet above ground, and a small coal furnace for heating water, which was used for cleaning the creamy cans. Vernon Davis remembers taking cream to the drop-off station on the way to school in 1925. The drop-off station was closed about 1936 when a Weyers Cave dairy opened and began picking up cream at the farm.

Foundation of the Augusta Dairy drop-off station

Shave and a Haircut, Two Bits

Minor Young's original barber shop

Nothing is known of the barbering trade in New Hope until the 1920s. We do know that there was a "Back Room" in the New Hope Garage and over the years a number of barbers used this area for a shop that was open for business on Saturday afternoons and Saturday nights.

Some of the men who cut hair in this shop were Howard Wiseman, father of Mac Wiseman, Mr. Wikel, Bill Baber, Ike Bryan, and several others whose names we can't remember. About 1944 Ike Bryan opened a full-time barber shop and shoe repair business in the Eddie Wine service station that had been closed for several years.

After World War II, Minor Young was discharged from the army and moved to New Hope in 1946. For several years he worked at some of the local industrial plants. In 1947 he bought from Paul Hunter a piece of land located north of New Hope of Route 608. He built a house on the property and in 1950 he constructed a small shop that served his barbering business until 1955 when he constructed a much larger cinderblock shop. He enlarged the shop in 1956 and again in 1964, the second time in order to provide room for his wife Katherine's beauty shop. The shop remained open until his death in 1979.

Minor and Katherine Young's barber and beauty shop after 1964

Community Fair

The New Hope Community Fair was a big day for the community and the surrounding area. Besides the many exhibits, there were activities for children. One of the big events was the bicycle race from the school house to Piedmont and back. A pie eating contest was another fun event. Unlike today's fairs, the New Hope Community fair had no rides. The one-day fair had no entry fee and exhibits were in field crops, vegetables, poultry, sheep, horses, swine, beef and dairy, canning, baking, fancy work, school work, and flowers. The exhibits were judged, ribbons were awarded for first, second, and third place and the cash prizes were varied from two dollars to twenty-five cents.

In 1935, fair sponsors included Leggett Department Store (Staunton), Staunton Furniture Company, Augusta Co-operative Farm Bureau, Staunton Coca-Cola Bottling Works, Staunton Creamery, Inc., The Young Man's Shop (Staunton), J.H. Leonard (Crimora), Frank McClure (Candidate for Commissioner of Revenue), Nicholas Milling Co., C.M. Drumheller's Service Station (New Hope), Harry Burnett (Candidate for County Clerk), E. M. Garber's Gene-

A 1935 fair program and a 1937 blue ribbon serve as reminders of the community fair.

Earl Wampler competes in a jousting tournament at Natural Chimneys while the children at right, Earl, Jr., Betty, and David Wampler, watch.

ral Merchandise, G. M. Gilkerson (Democratic Nominee for Sheriff), Robertson's Fertilizers (Staunton), K.L. Chapman (General Auctioneer), Riverside Hatchery (Grottoes), J.N. McFarland (Candidate for County Treasurer), East Side Service Station (Crimora), Bear Book Co. (Staunton), Dr. R. Guy Fisher (Eye, Ear, Nose, and Throat Specialist), Kennedy Drug Co., Ltd. (Staunton), Ft. Defiance Mills, Black's Auto Service (New Hope), Swift's Red Steer Fertilizer (Staunton), Eutsler Bros. (Grottoes), Valley Electric Company (Grottoes), Cross Road Service Station (New Hope), New Hope Garage, Red Mills Inc. (Crimora), J.C. Coiner (County Agent), Smith Douglas Company Inc. (Staunton), Southern Electric Co. (Staunton), Central Chemical Co. Inc. (Crimora), Willberger Funeral Home (New Hope), Busy Bee Restaurant (Staunton), J. W. Garber General Merchandise (Piedmont), and Mt. Meridan Service Station.

The biggest event of the fair was a jousting tournament. The riders with their horses would arrive by midmorning and take turns practicing for the afternoon event. Participants (called knights) came from Augusta and neighboring counties but local favorites were Earl Wampler and his son Earl, Jr. Earl Wampler was the driving force behind the New Hope Fair Jousting Tournament. When the contest was over, the winners were recognized and presented with a cash award. There was a food stand that served hot dogs, hamburgers, and cokes that were cooled in a wooden tub filled with ice.

The fair was first held in 1932 and was suspended at the beginning of World War II and never resumed after the war.

SOURCE: New Hope Fair Program, October 25, 1935.

Ruritan Club

The Mt. Clinton Ruritan Club sponsored the organizational meeting of the New Hope Ruritan Club on March 14, 1939. Membership applications were received from twenty-three people and six others were added to the list. The first regular meeting of the club was held April 13, 1939, and New Hope was presented the seventy-fifth charter. Officers elected at this meeting were: President, J. L. Shaver; Vice President, J. D. Kramer; Secretary, E. W. Spitzer; Treasurer, David Geiman; Chorister, Joe Humbert; Sergeant-At-Arms, N.C. Guynn; Chaplain, S. A. Harley; Directors, one year, J. E. Wampler, two years, E. C. Geiman, three years, J. L. Driver.

Among the activities the club sponsored during the remainder of 1939 were: a community Bible School, a community Christmas tree, purchasing a piano for the school, and presenting a play. Over the years, the club aided people who were ill, needy, or misfortunate. As early as 1941, there was an interest in forming a Boy Scout Troop and the troop was finally organized in 1951. During World War II, the club was busy in bond drives, giving blood, and holding first aid classes. The Ruritan Club was instrumental in getting street lights for the village during 1949. In 1951, the community found itself without the services of a doctor. The Health Committee determined that, if the community wanted a doctor, it must provide a place for him to live and an office. Early in 1952, a lot was purchased on which to build a medical center for the community. Three Ruritan members were appointed trustees, plans were drawn for a building, the building was dedicated on Sunday afternoon, August 1952, and Dr. William T. Davis moved in the following week. This was the largest project the Ruritan Club had undertaken and the cost for the building, lot, and equipment was $23,000.

The club has sponsored many money raising projects, given plays and minstrels, and held shooting matches, community sales, ball tournaments, cake walks, baby shows, and beauty contests. In 1960, the club organized the Little League ball team and the Babe Ruth team in 1968. To advance youth and community activities, lights were added to the school grounds in 1964 and a concession stand in 1968. These ball field facilities have been continuously upgraded over the years, including a major modernization in 1979 and 1987. In 1963, the work of a club committee resulted in the organization of the Pine Bluff Parks, Inc., a swim and recreation park. The New Hope Club sponsored the Crimora Club, chartered May 8, 1953, and the Barren Ridge Annex Club, chartered January 8, 1968. For many years the club has helped support Augusta Expoland in Fishersville by contributing to the 4-H/FFA Market Livestock Show and Sale. Since 1986, the club has sought to foster interest in a New Hope Fire Department. The club provided leadership, which resulted in the initial fund drive and the formation of the New Hope Volunteer Fire Department in 1990.

During its first half century (1939-1989) the New Hope Ruritan Club contributed substantially to the community. In fifty years there have been some 600 monthly meetings where good food has always been accompanied by good fellowship. Community service has been the focus of the club and much has been accomplished while many fine active members have made their marks and gone on. The New Hope Ruritan Club does not rest on past achievements, and members are challenged to worthwhile community service and to remain a catalyst for unified local spirit.

SOURCE: Based on a summary of the New Hope Ruritan Club Minutes compiled by Lawrence Hildebrand, 2004.

Boy Scouts of America, Troop 86

On June 6, 1951, twelve Boy Scouts got their certificates of membership and New Hope Troop 86 received a charter from the Boy Scouts of America at a service in the New Hope Elementary School auditorium. The new troop was officially marked by the presence of Roy D. Ridgeway, executive, Stonewall Jackson Area Council BSA, who congratulated the boys and gave them an encouraging talk.

George W. Swartz was the first scoutmaster of the troop, which was sponsored by the New Hope Ruritan Club. Assistant scoutmaster was K. L. Chapman, Jr. and Charles Quick, Jr. was junior assistant scoutmaster. The troop's first scouts were Curtis Coffman, Donnie Rankin, Johnny Wise, Bill Evers, Cary Spitzer, Frank Drumheller, Alvin Rosen, Ray Drumheller, Stoney Quick, Donald Painter, Fred Swartz, and John Ocheltree.

The troop has been strong for the past fifty-five years and is proud that thirty-eight boys have advanced to the rank of Eagle Scout. The Ruritan Club continues as a sponsoring organization and the troop has remained very active under the excellent leadership of Scoutmaster Mark Howdyshell, who sadly passed away in 2006.

The New Hope Boy Scouts have helped develop a lot of good men. Among the Eagle Scouts pictured on the next page are two ministers, a veterinarian, a school administrator, and a businessman.

SOURCE: Interview with Bobby Kester, 2005 and Boy Scout Troop 86 records

Scoutmasters

G. W. Swartz	1951-1956	Dennis Davis	1975-1980
Owen Harner	1957-1963	Robert Kilmer	1981-1989
Albert E. Propst	1964-1971	Edwin Zwart	1990-1991
Charles F. Wertman	1972	John Flora	1992-1996
Ray C. Wright	1973-1974	Mark Howdyshell	1997-2006 (deceased)

New Hope Scouting, 2001: (l-r) Kelly Chapman, Ray Drumheller, Frank Drumheller, Andrew Kester, Fred Swartz, John Wise, and Curtis Coffman.

Eagle Scouts

Fred Swartz	1954	Brian Kilmer	1990
Jimmy Hawkins	1963	Rod Diehl	1990
John Sandridge	1963	Nickolas Paynter	1996
Dennis Davis	1973	Andrew Kester	1997
Greg Bean	1974	William B. Harner III	1998
Steve Davis	1974	Noah Early	1998
John Flora	1974	Timothy Howdyshell	1999
Steven Marks	1974	Ryan Kester	1999
Dan Flora	1977	Jonathan Paynter	1999
John S. Sjostrom, Jr.	1977	Adam Early	2000
Steve Carter	1978	Drew T. Dunsmore	2001
Alan Meadows	1978	Isaac C. Rickman	2001
Mark Davis	1978	Patrick Paynter	2001
Walley Smith	1979	Scott Adam	2001
Richard D. Hurwitz, Jr.	1982	Kevin Hitt	2002
Raymond Kilmer	1983	Matthew Stephen	2003
Daniel Miller	1986	Owen Wimer	2005

New Hope Scoutmasters past and present in 2001 (front l-r): Richard Booth (assistant), Robert Kilmer, Owen Harner; (back l-r) Mark Howdyshell, Ray Wright, Dennis Davis, and Al Propst.

Local Celebrities
Malcolm (Mac) Wiseman, Country Music Legend

Mac Wiseman

Mac Wiseman was born and grew up in the Crimora area of Augusta County. He attended the Harriston Elementary School and graduated from New Hope High School in 1943. During his four years of high school, he was a member of the Science, Beta, and Glee Clubs. He served one year as president of the Beta Club. He often entertained the students at assembly programs and other times with his playing and singing.

After high school, he attended Shenandoah Conservatory of Music at Dayton, Virginia (now Shenandoah University in Winchester, Virginia). By 1943, World War II had taken many of the men into service. Radio Station WSVA needed a program director, and Mac was hired before he finished his studies at Shenandoah Conservatory of Music. While at WSVA, he served as announcer, disc jockey, and entertainer. As his popularity grew, he moved to Richmond, Virginia; Wheeling, West Virginia; and Knoxville, Tennessee.

Mac's biggest selling songs include: "Love Letters in the Sand" released in 1954, "Tis Sweet to Be Remembered" from 1951 and "Davy Crockett." In the 1950s, Mac regularly played 300 one-night shows a year. A talent for playing the guitar and singing led Mac around the world. He has performed at places including the Rose Bowl, Japan, Germany, England, and Switzerland. In 1980, he played in ten countries with singers Johnny Cash and Jerry Lee Lewis. The smallest crowd the group played to was 25,000 people.

Mac was one of the founders of the Country Music Association and is in the Country Music Hall of Fame in Nashville. He thinks the reason for the longevity of his material is because it is traditional. The music and songs have been handed down from generation to generation, plus they are a slice of life. As a child Mac was afflicted with polio that left him with a limp, but this has never hampered his career.

SOURCE: Biographical information provided by Malcolm Wiseman, 2005.

Dell Curry, One of the Purest Shooters

Dell Curry was born and grew up in the Harriston area. He attended elementary school in New Hope and played Little League baseball and basketball at New Hope. At an early age it was obvious that his ability and skills were more advanced than the other kids. At Fort Defiance High School, he was a four-year starter for Coach Don Landes' basketball teams. During Dell's sophomore year, the team went 27-0, and won the Virginia State Championship. During his high school career, the basketball team lost only ten games.

Dell is the kind of person that any community would be proud to claim as its own. During his senior year, he received the 1982 Dilettoso Award at a banquet at the Staunton Elks Lodge, where he made a surprise announcement. "Since I have a full scholarship to Virginia Tech, I would like to share my good fortune with the runner-up in the voting, Andrew Taylor of Riverheads," he said in forgoing the $300 scholarship given the winner each year by the Jaycees. "I just want to give the scholarship to you," Curry said in handing the check to Taylor. "That is just the way Dell is, a super individual," his coach Don Landes said.

Dell received many honors in his four years at Fort Defiance High School (Class of 1982) and was recruited by a number of large colleges and universities, but ended speculation in early December by verbally committing to Virginia Tech. He became the first basketball player from Augusta County to be invited to play in the McDonald's Classic at Capital Centre in Landover, Maryland. This honor was topped when he was invited and played in McDonald's All-America game in Chicago where he led his team in scoring. Curry was named to Scholastic and Parade High School All-America basketball teams.

At Virginia Tech, Dell had four outstanding years

Dell Curry at Fort Defiance

Dell Curry at Virginia Tech

as a starter and was an All-America two years. After college, he was drafted into the NBA by the Utah Jazz. He spent sixteen very successful seasons in the NBA playing for five different teams. He was considered one of the purest shooters in the game.

Dell is now retired from the NBA and lives in Charlotte, North Carolina, with his wife and three children. He serves as Director of Player Relations with the Charlotte Hornets. Dell is very active in the community and has established the Dell Curry Foundation for underprivileged children.

Recent Developments

For the first half of the twentieth century, New Hope was a charming and clean rural village of 200 plus people. There were no factories, so it became a bedroom community for Waynesboro, where DuPont, Wayne Manufacturing, Crompton, and other plants employed many of New Hope's residents. The forty-plus wood frame houses were well kept; most were nicely painted and had a garden, a chicken house, a hog pen, and a white picket fence. The village boasted a doctor, many successful farmers, several highly respected teachers, a successful flour miller, and many other accomplished people. There were two thriving general merchandise stores, a switchboard association or telephone company, an elementary and high school, a funeral service, and two garages. New Hope was practically self-contained in the sense that most needs could be satisfied locally. Exceptions included the Staunton Creamery or Early Dawn Dairy, which delivered milk to each house, and dry cleaners, which picked up and delivered clothes. New Hope was like many small towns or villages in America; the people were friendly and industrious, and it was a nice place to live and rear a family.

A *Waynesboro News Virginian* article dated February 8, 1951, described New Hope as follows. "Each home looks spotless, each yard is free of trash, and the streets are very clean. Even the school grounds, where candy and gum wrappers and scrap paper are usually found, are free of these items. . . . Picket fences, which surround a majority of the homes, are painted a gleaming white. Everything is as neat as the proverbial pin."

During the second half of the twentieth century, New Hope began to decline. In 1947, New Hope High School consolidated with four or five other county schools and became known as Wilson Memorial High School. The elementary school remained at New Hope until it was consolidated at Fort Defiance in 1995. When self-service supermarkets came to Waynesboro, people began to shop there for groceries and other needs and by the 1970s both general stores had closed. What was known as the New Hope General Merchandise Store was bulldozed about 1980, and the New Hope Garage closed about 1975. The New Hope Bank was acquired by Jefferson Bank of Charlottesville about 1970 and was closed about 1995 by Wachovia Bank. In 1952, New Hope dedicated a new Medical Center and handed the keys to the building over to Dr. William T. Davis. In 1965, the Medical Center was closed when Dr. Theron R. Rolston, Jr., moved and the community was unable to attract a new doctor. A new post office was built in 1965; it was the only new public building in New Hope in many years. However, the New Hope area has made some improvements or upgrades. Augusta County brought sewer service to New Hope in the 1980s but decided not to bring water, so each home still uses wells or cisterns. The Methodist Church was expanded and improved and the Church of the Brethren built a new building.

New Hope United Methodist Church, third building, photo taken 1990

Middle River Church of the Brethren, fourth building, photo taken 2005

Volunteer Fire Department

The New Hope Volunteer Fire Department was established in 1990 when the community expressed the need after a person had to be rescued by a passer-by during a house fire. At the time of the fire, the fire companies who served the area had so far to travel that the house was engulfed in flame when they arrived. Members of the community got together with Augusta County and addressed the concerns. The county helped by donating a used engine to get the department started. The school board gave the property for the first firehouse which began in the old agricultural building at the New Hope School. The building had no running water or restrooms; it had one office and a storage room. The equipment consisted of a 1954 GMC fire engine and a 1974 Chevrolet salvage truck. The first fire chief was Gerald Early. He held that office for five years until he resigned. In 1990, the forty-five members ran a total of eighty-five emergency calls.

New Hope's first firehouse and fire truck, 1990

The list of charter members included:

Walter Abbott	Judi Garber	Bob Morrison
Steve Bowman	Tim Hensley	Paul O'Gorek
Mark Bryant	Scott Hildebrand	George Potter
Charlie Cline	Harry Krista	Vince Schindler
Lester Courtney	David Laymen	Lee Smallwood
Martin Drumheller	John Laymen	Eddie Thornton
Gerald Early	Roger Layman	Eddie Zwart

In 1991, the New Hope Fire Department added first responder service. During the first five years, the department purchased a lot of used equipment due to financial constraints. The company purchased an engine from the Grottoes Fire Department, an engine from the Bridgewater Fire Department, and equipment from other agencies.

Rankin Station, home of the New Hope Volunteer Fire Department, built 1999

Lester Courtney was elected New Hope Fire Chief in 1995. The department started working to build a new building and partnered with the New Hope Ruritan Club. The Houff Corporation donated the money to complete the building in recognition of the Rankin family who lived in the area. The building, which is named Rankin Station, was completed in 1999. A five-year plan was established and the department started upgrading equipment. A 1989 Grumman fire engine was purchased from the New Market Fire Department. In 2000, the department purchased a 2000 Chevrolet brush truck which was used as a multipurpose unit that would run brush fires and rescue calls. For personal reasons, Chief Lester Courtney had to step down in December 2000.

In 2001, Greg Schacht accepted and is currently holding the office of chief. In that year, the New Hope Volunteer Fire Department purchased a new 2001 New Lexington fire engine. This was a major accomplishment for the department. Also in 2001, the department started the EMS (Emergency Medical Service) transport service. This was instituted after conducting a community survey to determine what services were needed to better assist the community. The department saw a need for an ambulance service. With help from the Staunton-Augusta Rescue Squad, Waynesboro Rescue, and Grottoes Rescue, this was accomplished. In 2002, the New Hope Volunteer Fire Department asked the county for career personnel to assist in running calls during the daylight hours to enhance the services to the New Hope community. The county responded by hiring three persons trained at the advanced life support level.

During 2003, the New Hope Volunteer Fire Department ran a total of 916 emergency calls. In 2003, the department ordered a new ambulance, which was delivered in March 2004. The department was also awarded a grant to purchase another new ambulance for 2004.

SOURCE: Based on a letter from Greg Schacht, Chief of the New Hope Volunteer Fire Department, Inc., 2004.

Dedicated June 12, 1999, in memory of Walter and Sadie Rankin with members of the Rankin family present at the dedication.

Looking Forward

Past and Present Views

A view of New Hope from the west, circa 1907. By the beginning of the twentieth century, New Hope had developed into a thriving community. In this photo, one can see (l-r) the Willberger bank barn, Stout-Fretwell-Garber General Store, the Fretwell-Garber House, the Crawford-Willberger Store, the Dickerson-Fretwell Tavern, Roberts-Obenschain barn and several other houses.

A view of New Hope from the west, 2005. As evidenced by the above 2005 view of the village, not much has changed in New Hope during the past 100 years. From left to right the Willberger bank barn is still there, and the Fretwell House is visible. The Bank of New Hope building is visible, but it was not constructed until 1913. The Stout-Fretwell-Garber General Store is not visible because the building was bulldozed around 1980. The Fretwell-Garber House is still there along with the Crawford-Willberger Store. The Dickerson-Fretwell Tavern (with addition) remains and is now the home of Isabell Willberger. The other houses still remain and are occupied.

A view of New Hope from the south, 1907 (top) and 2005. In this view of New Hope from the south it is apparent that more has changed. From left to right, we see that the Town Hall building is gone, but Dr. Fisher's house remains, and his office is now present. The Myers-Bauserman (Blacksmith) Shop is gone as is the James White House. The United Methodist Church remains on the hill and Dr. Miller's house remains. In the foreground are houses and outbuildings built during the past eighty years.

Since its heyday in the nineteenth century, New Hope has lost much of its traffic and former prosperity. The twentieth-century decline of this small village has led to the closing of most commercial businesses. The consolidation of schools has left the New Hope schoolhouse vacant. Many nineteenth-century frame and log houses do remain in the older portion of the village and illustrate the various types of construction popular in the surrounding area throughout the century. Most of the post-WWI construction occurred north of town along Route 608. In the mid-1990s, a number of new homes were built on the west side of 608 north of the town.

New Hope Rates Dot on Map

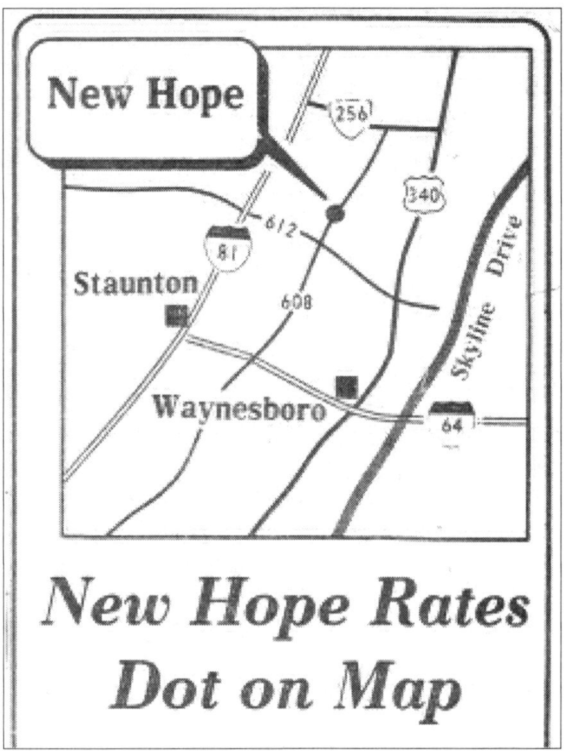

As we look forward into the twenty-first century, it is unclear what the future holds for New Hope, but we do know that New Hope rates a dot on the map. According to Gary Robertson of the *Richmond Times-Dispatch* "after nearly 200 years of obscurity, the tiny Augusta County hamlet of New Hope will finally be getting its place in the sun – or, rather, its place on the state highway map." In 1981, the New Hope Ruritan Club worked to get the community of about 400 on the map. William S. Miller wrote the state highway commissioner and told him "that New Hope was a thriving community thriving in a small way, perhaps, but still thriving – and we thought we deserved to have our name on the map." The highway official agreed, and New Hope is now included on Virginia's highway map.

Future Vision

Over the past 200 years of its existence, New Hope has contributed in many important ways to the development of Augusta County and the Valley. Its history needs to be preserved and a preservation plan needs to be developed for its built resources. A few historical resources like the Stout-Fretwell-Garber General Store and the antebellum Stout-McCauley House have already been lost and others are threatened. Fortunately, some of New Hope's early families are still represented in the community and they may prove to be a great asset by helping to kindle a preservation spirit.

The authors hope that this book will help create some public awareness of New Hope's past heritage and its valuable historical resources. Preservation initiatives by residents are needed to save the many houses, farm buildings, and other built resources in the area.

As we look forward, the vision for New Hope must be determined by the community and it is probable that New Hope will not want to become a center of commercial development. The vision may be to remain a small, quiet farming village that is proud of its past, hopeful of its future, and determined to preserve and protect its historical resources. If this were to be New Hope's future, it would be a good future indeed.

Bibliography and Sources

1. Barnett, Marie, letter from Allen E. Roberts Masonic Library and Museum of Virginia, Inc., August 22, 2005.
2. Barnhart, Nathaniel G., *Barnhart Family History, Augusta County, Virginia, 1767-1967.*
3. Barnhart, Nathaniel G., *United Methodist Church History, 1806–1972, New Hope, Virginia.*
4. Battle of Piedmont from website www.cr.nps.gov/hps/abpp/shenandoah/svs3-9.html.
5. Brice, Marshall M., *Map of the Battle of Piedmont, Conquest of a Valley.*
6. Certificate of Incorporation of The Bank of New Hope, Incorporation 1913 provided by B.F. Caricofe, Jr.
7. Chataigne, *Augusta County, Virginia Gazetteer and Classified Business Directory*, 1888
8. "Field Infirmary, Augusta Co.," *Staunton Spectator,* August 21, 1864.
9. Coffman, W. Paul, *A History of Middle River Congregation, Church of the Brethren*, 1964.
10. Coffman, Ralph S., Eagle Graveyard, November 14, 1952.
11. Coffman, Ralph S. Old Myers Graveyard, March 29, 1967.
12. Constitution and Bylaws of the New Hope Switchboard Association adopted October 25, 1902.
13. Corporate Minutes of the Bank of New Hope, 1913-1928.
14. Correspondence from the Commonwealth of Virginia, Banking Division, 1913.
15. Dixon, Walter, "The James Allen Families of Early Augusta County," *Magazine of Virginia Genealogy*, Volume 42, Number 1.
16. Flory, Earl D., (compiled) *East Augusta Mutual Fire Insurance Co., Organization and Growth, 1870-1970.*
17. History of the Bank of New Hope from Corporate Minutes of the Bank of New Hope, 1913-1928.
18. Herndon, Scioto M., Middle River Graveyard, Library of Virginia, August 12, 1936.
19. Herndon, Scioto M., New Hope Cemetery, Library of Virginia, August 12, 1936.
20. Herndon, Scioto M., Humbert Graveyard, Library of Virginia, August 12, 1936.
21. Hildebrand, Lawrence, Summary of the New Hope Ruritan Club, 2004.
22. Hotchkiss, Jed., "Plan of New Hope Village," *Historical Atlas of Augusta County, Virginia*, 1885.
23. Interview conducted with Catherine Garber Crist, daughter of Minor Garber, at her house in Harrisonburg, Virginia, on January 15, 2004.
24. Kester, Bobby, New Hope Boy Scout Troop 86 record.
25. Knightly Light & Power Co. Subscription Memorandum provided to Wayne Garber by Catherine Garber Crist on February 21, 2004.
26. MacMaster, Richard, *Augusta County History, 1865-1950.*
27. May, C. E., *My Augusta*, 1987.
28. McCleary, Ann, "Eighteenth Century to the Present, Historic Landmarks of Virginia" (now Department of Historic Resources), 1982.
29. Minutes of the New Hope Town Council, April 5, 1890, to December 12, 1911, provided by B. F. Caricofe, Jr.

30. Minutes of the New Hope Switchboard Association, 1902 to 1919.
31. New Hope Fair Program, October 25, 1935.
32. Nutt, Joe, "Kerr House," *Daily News Leader*, October 28, 1992.
33. Nutt, Joe, "Belmont Plantation/Beard House," *Daily News Leader*, September 22, 1993.
34. Nutt, Joe, "More on Mills: Tilt-Hammer and Others," *Daily News Leader*, September 1992
35. Nutt, Joe, information entitled "Black Oak Spring/Rutledge-Mehler House"
36. Obituary of Dr. Clarence P. Obenschain from *Staunton News Leader.*
37. Obituary of Dr. William Franklin Stout from *Staunton News Leader.*
38. Obituary of Dr. Thomas C. Miller from *Staunton News Leader.*
39. Obituary of Dr. Theron Rice Rolston from *Staunton News Leader.*
40. Railroad information from website trainweb.org/varail/shen.html
41. Schacht, Greg, letter regarding the New Hope Volunteer Fire Department, Inc., 2004.
42. Shaver, M. H., letter entitled "What We Did on Wednesday after the Piedmont Battle, June 8, 1864."
43. Shaver, M. H., letter entitled "Letter Written After the Battle of Piedmont."
44. Simmons, Sue, "Teacher Recalls School's Early Days," *Augusta Country*, May 1995 (Vol. 2, Issue 5)
45. *Staunton News Leader* article August 12, 1952, regarding Dr. William T. Davis.
46. Stephenson, Roy, "Ancient Mill Moved To Michie Tavern," *Staunton News Leader,* 1975.
47. Willberger, Isabell, provided copies of the following Civil War letters: Letter from Civil War Soldier Staying in Fretwell Tavern, Letter of Response from David Wall's Wife to Mr. W. D. Greenway, and Letter from David Wall's Wife to Mr. Fretwell.
48. Willberger, Isabell, provided information regarding Willberger Funeral Service, 2005.
49. Wiseman, Malcolm, biographical information provided, 2005.

About the Authors

Owen Early Harner is a native of New Hope, having been born and reared in the village. He is a graduate of New Hope High School and attended Davis & Elkins College, where he majored in physical education. He taught the sixth grade at Crimora Elementary School for ten years and has resided in the New Hope area all his adult life. Owen and Dolly, his wife, have five children and fourteen grandchildren. He retired from DuPont as a laboratory supervisor, where he worked for twenty-seven years. Owen has an abiding interest in the history and heritage of New Hope and has collected information and photographs over the past fifty years.

Wayne Edward Garber is a native of Virginia's Shenandoah Valley. He lived in New Hope during the first eight years of his life and attended first and second grade at New Hope Elementary School. In 1952, Wayne's family moved to a farm near Waynesboro, Virginia, where he grew up. He was a member of the Middle River Church of the Brethren until he was eleven years old. He graduated in 1962 from Wilson Memorial High School and in 1966 from Virginia Tech with a degree in business administration. He was a human resources management professional for twenty-eight years and for seven years operated Wayne Garber & Associates, a retained executive search firm. Wayne and Gail, his wife, live in Williamsburg, Virginia, and have two children and two grandchildren. Wayne has an interest in genealogy and has written a family history entitled *Johannes "John H." Garber (1732-1783), A Branch of His Descendants.*

Owen Harner, left, and Wayne Garber

Index

D

E

F

G

H

T

V

W

Y

Z